# UNION INSTITUTE & UNIVERSITY AT 50:

*leaders realizing a dream*

Union Institute & University at 50: Leaders Realizing a Dream
*by Benjamin R. Justesen*

Copyright © 2015 by Union Institute & University
book design by Lucy Swerdfeger — published by
New Education Press, Scottsdale, Arizona

ISBN: 978-1-93284283-8 — $ 14.95

All rights reserved. No part of this book may be used
or reproduced in any manner whatsoever without written
permission from the publisher, except in the case of
brief quotations embodied in articles and reviews.

NewEducationPress.Com
*published in the United States of America*

# UNION INSTITUTE & UNIVERSITY AT 50: *leaders realizing a dream*

Benjamin R. Justesen

# Union Institute & University at 50:
*leaders realizing a dream*

Foreword — vii

Introduction and Acknowledgments — ix

Prelude: The Goddard Example — 1

Chapter 1: The Union is Born — 9

Chapter 2: The Baskin Era — 25

Chapter 3: The Interim Era of King V. Cheek and Kenneth W. Rothe — 57

Chapter 4: The Conley Era — 77

Chapter 5: Transitional Leaders Mervyn L. Cadwallader and Judith A. Sturnick — 95

Chapter 6: Entering the Modern Era: Roger H. Sublett — 113

Epilogue: The Union Legacy in the Outside World — 137

Centers Around The Country — 142

Appendix A: Current Trustees — 145

Appendix B: Board Chairs, 1965–2014 — 149

Appendix C: Members of the Board of Trustees, 1971–2015 — 151

Bibliography — 173

Endnotes — 181

*From the Chair of the Board of Trustees*

# FOREWORD

We have just completed a yearlong celebration of Union Institute & University's first fifty years. We celebrated with events in almost every location across the country, focusing on the people who make up Union's unique legacy. While we could not feature all 15,500 of our esteemed graduates and the great work they are doing, several made presentations and led discussions. They shared their knowledge, experience, and expertise, and took time to speak to the many dreams and accomplishments of all our alumni who work hard every day to make their communities better for all of us. Some earn national recognition, some receive regional or local recognition, and some may be recognized only within their own families, but it is all important work and all of us at Union are proud of this.

In one sense, the fiftieth anniversary and this book are a bridge between the past and the future. One of our events included a panel of five of the almost twenty alumni who have served as presidents of other colleges. These men and women spoke about the future of higher education, all the challenges and opportunities, and what we can expect to see. Doesn't that seem appropriate to be a part of Union's celebration?

Of course, we of Union have had our debates and discussions over the years, some of which is mentioned in the pages herein. I actually find these exchanges to be a sign of Union's health and tenacity to survive. Healthy institutions—

particularly academic institutions—should be places in which new ideas are given birth, debated, discussed (sometimes heatedly) and then agreed to, rejected, or left on the table for further discussion. The many trustees and the presidents who have served Union over the years (and are listed in the book) deserve recognition for their service and vision in leading this institution through thick and thin.

In addition to the leadership, many others have worked—and continue to strive—in support of Union. Our faculty and staff should frequently and daily receive heartfelt recognition. These individuals make it all happen, and do it day after day, day-in and day-out.

On behalf the board of trustees and leadership of Union, past and present, I thank you all. Finally, I know I speak for the entire community when I invite you to be proud of "Your Union" and to enjoy this history.

Donald J. Feldmann, **CHAIR OF THE BOARD**, 2014–2015

*From the President*

## INTRODUCTION AND ACKNOWLEDGMENTS

Union Institute & University was founded during the tumultuous 1960s, a time of change and transformation throughout all sectors and in all facets of our society. Looking back, 1964 was a pivotal year for our nation and our culture. The nation was still grieving the death of JFK; the Civil Rights Act of 1964 became law and Lyndon Johnson declared war on poverty. Dr. Martin Luther King, Jr. won the Nobel Peace Prize; Nelson Mandela was sentenced to life in prison in South Africa; Congress authorized war against North Vietnam leading to the student protest movement; and James Meredith graduated from the University of Mississippi as the first African-American to attend a segregated school. The Beatles arrived in the United States for the first time and the first Ford Mustangs came off the assembly line. Betty Friedan's *The Feminine Mystique* was released as a paperback, with its first printing selling 1.4 million copies. A loaf of bread cost twenty cents, a stamp was five cents, and smoking was determined to be a health hazard by the Surgeon General. *Jeopardy* and *Bewitched* began on television, while *Dr. Strangelove*, *Goldfinger*, and *Mary Poppins* premiered at the movies.

It was during this time of upheaval that ten university presidents gathered in Vermont with a mission to change the face of higher education. They established a consortium of colleges and universities called the Union for Research and Experimentation in Higher Education, a forward-facing institution formed for three reasons: 1) to foster cooperative efforts in experimentation and research among the member colleges; 2) to encourage experimentation and research by faculty; and 3) to disseminate information through conferences and publications regarding the Union's activities.

These visionary leaders glimpsed the future. They pioneered many of the concepts now common in higher education including non-residential learning, credit for prior experience and knowledge, and learner-centered education, especially for adults. They created the concept of distance education and flexible delivery models, understanding the model of online education before the technology existed to support the approach.

While much has changed throughout the last fifty years—including Union's name, its reach, and its offerings—one thing has stayed true: the belief that education is about many facets of the human experience. Education is about achieving aspirations and goals, celebrating the very best of the human spirit, expanding knowledge, and transforming lives and communities.

Union Institute & University has had a remarkable journey. Yet, the Union has not told its story in this one book. When we began planning the fiftieth anniversary celebration for 2014, we decided it was time to chronicle the history of this unique institution in a brief, readable volume. Because of this, we have not attempted to tell all of the stories—and certainly were not able to include all of the players who were part of our history and development. Nevertheless, I hope that we have succeeded in painting a picture of Union's auspicious beginnings, bringing light its very early days and adding the evolving dimension as Union continued to develop over the years.

Dr. Benjamin Justesen has done an excellent job in capturing the Union's past. His in-depth research included notable conversations with many figures of the past, as well as the review of copious documents and materials about Union. As he conducted interviews with the five surviving presidents, Ben Justesen elected to organize his work around the history of Union's leadership. This arrangement does not mean that he and all of us do not recognize the tremendous work of Union's faculty members and administration, both past and present, along with staff members who served throughout the institution's many years with distinction and determination. In gratitude, this volume is dedicated to all who have served Union Institute & University since 1964.

Having served as president since 2003, I have been amazed by the impressive work of Union's graduates across the globe over the last 50 years. Many have been scholars who opened doors to new ideas, new innovations, new institutions, and, in fact, different ways of thinking and knowing. It has been wonderful to be a part of this experimenting community.

I express our collective thanks to Ben Justesen for capturing the essence of Union's spirit over the last fifty years. Also, we acknowledge the contribution of $100,000 by a local anonymous foundation for its generous support of Union's fiftieth anniversary celebration and the publication of this history.

For helping Union mark its golden anniversary and celebrate its history, thanks goes to The Most Honorable Portia Simpson-Miller, Prime Minister of Jamaica and a graduate of Union's bachelor's program (1997), who was a star attraction when she spoke on Union's behalf in Miami, in June 2014; to Dr. Ken Dychtwald (PhD 1976), founder of AgeWave, who wowed a large audience in Cincinnati, with his dynamic presentation on the aging boom; and Major General Sharon Dunbar (ret.), a 32-year military veteran who shared her insights and observations with Union's 2014 California graduates in August 2014 and was bestowed with an honorary doctorate. All three were wonderful participants in the life of Union this last year.

Union also hosted a forum about the changing face of higher education, keynoted by five of Union's many alums who have served as presidents at numerous colleges around the country. I thank Dr. George Pruitt, Dr. Scott Miller, Dr. Mark Schulman, Dr. Judy Walters, and Dr. Gary Wheeler for their insightful presentations. The 2014 year was notable as it allowed Union to reflect and celebrate its past, and, more importantly, it provided the historical context with which we may also look forward toward Union's next fifty years.

On behalf of Union, I sincerely acknowledge Union's board of trustees, named later in these pages, who gave financial, vocal, and active support to our fiftieth anniversary year. Special recognition goes to 50th Anniversary celebration co-chairs Mr. Don Feldmann, chair of Union's board and Dr. Gladys Hankins, alumna and trustee, for their tireless involvement in the planning and support of our celebrations. I also thank Vice President for Advancement Carolyn Krause and her staff for their leadership in implementing the numerous year-long activities and celebrations. I acknowledge Union's International Alumni Association Board, under the leadership of Dr. Neal Meier, along with alumni Dr. Steven Swerdfeger and Dr. Don Kagin, who participated actively in Union's fiftieth celebration with its 50/50 Campaign and Auction.

Of course, to our many friends and colleagues around the country who participated in the celebrations as they continued day-to-day contributions to the school, I extend my deepest appreciation for your involvement in the life of Union. Without the assistance of all of the above, it would not have been possible to have completed our fiftieth-anniversary journey so successfully.

It continues to be my pleasure to serve as president of this unique university. Enjoy this brief history that recognizes countless pioneers in higher education, many of whom preceded us at Union. What a remarkable legacy they have left, and what an amazing institution their collective genius has created.

Roger H. Sublett, PhD, **President**

*"College should provide educational opportunities for adults because learning should continue throughout life...."* [1]

## PRELUDE: THE GODDARD EXAMPLE

As 1963 dawned, Royce Stanley Pitkin—better known as "Tim" to his friends and much of the U.S. educational community—had one more dream to fulfill. An ambitious experiment to top all his previous experiments, educationally speaking, implementing this dream would require other players—other colleges with as much imagination as possible. Of course, it would also take money, and time. And not everyone he approached would agree that the time was even right for this experiment.

But Pitkin had never let inertia or doubts stand in his way. The longtime president of Vermont's Goddard College was then celebrating the twenty-fifth anniversary of the school he had helped rescue from oblivion just before World War II. What better way to mark such an anniversary than to spread the creative ferment that had come to symbolize Goddard's revitalized mentality and legacy?

In 1963, Tim Pitkin was nearing the age when many men of his generation were considering retirement, or at least slowing down to catch their breath. But so far he showed no sign of his age. The 62-year-old Pitkin, in fact, seemed as youthful as ever—he would head Goddard until the end of the decade, and work up until his death in 1986—and his philosophy always remained refreshingly innovative, his work ethic legendary.

The conference that Pitkin planned for his Plainfield campus at the end of the winter would be a daring springboard. From this conference, and a subsequent gathering in 1964, the new experimental union of like-minded schools would take root as Pitkin's offspring, forming the kernel of what would one day become the independent Union Institute & University.

Tim Pitkin had graduated from Goddard Seminary in 1919 before initially training in agriculture at the University of Vermont. In the late 1920s and early 1930s, during both the worst economic depression and farmland drought the nation had ever known, Pitkin altered his course. He started at Columbia University's graduate school, where his mentor was Dr. William Heard Kilpatrick, a follower of the Dewey model of progressive education. Fundamental to this model is the belief that interactive, self-directed education could help build civil, democratic societies. By 1933, when Pitkin had completed his PhD in education under Kilpatrick's wing, he had emerged as a confirmed innovator, seeking to "mend the rift between daily life and learning," as one chronicler later put it.[2]

Two years later, Pitkin returned as director of the new Goddard Junior College. But both the small school and its venerable parent were nearly defunct. The struggling College and its dwindling Seminary—eclipsed by the widespread availability of cheaper public high schools in an era of tight budgets—were faced with time-sensitive dilemmas carrying nearly insurmountable enrollment challenges: how to attract enough students to stay open in the short term, how to redefine the school's mission and attract more students in the medium term, and how to compete with far cheaper public colleges in the long term.

The answer required radical life-saving surgery on his beloved institution. Within a year of his return, Dr. Pitkin had become the president of both schools—and an avowed proponent of the conclusions reached in a study conducted by the Goddard faculty with Pitkin's encouragement. The study had pointed toward one inevitable conclusion: in order to survive in the ruthless world of modern education, Goddard would have to change its image and almost everything about the educational experience it offered its students. In effect, Goddard would have to be born again as a brand-new school.

Goddard's trustees agreed. But just what kind of school should it become? A conference in New York City, pushed by Pitkin, brought his old mentor, Dr. Kilpatrick, onto the Goddard stage. By March 1938, the new Goddard College was officially born—on a new campus in nearby Plainfield, Vermont. The school's first catalog proposed the education of both men and women for real living through the acknowledgment of real-life problems. This fundamental proposition became known as the Goddard College Philosophy, with its four deceptively simple guiding principles:

| 1 | Thought should be tested by action |
| 2 | We only learn what we can inwardly accept |
| 3 | One matures by carrying responsibilities suited to one's capacities |
| 4 | College should provide educational opportunities for adults because learning should continue throughout life.[3] |

Pitkin and his Goddard colleagues swiftly dispensed with everything that most mainstream schools believed were absolutely necessary for learning—grades, written examinations, required courses, credits, fraternities, athletics, honor rolls, and diplomas. In its place, they began creating an institution in which students, through community government and a daily work program, were in large part responsible for maintaining the campus and for developing policies that directly affected their lives. The result was the establishment of an experimental and innovative educational institution that made significant contributions to higher education.

Chartered in 1863 as a Universalist seminary, Green Mountain Central Institute initially began by offering high-school coursework and gradually evolved to become a feeder school for such colleges as Tufts University in Medford, Massachusetts. The seminary had always exemplified the inclusive, socially engaged values of its community. Now, in transforming the failing Goddard of old into the new, modern Goddard College, chartered in 1938, Pitkin sought to unite the liberal values of the Seminary with Dewey's belief in the link between education and more civil and democratic societies.

Pitkin channeled Dewey, setting Goddard on the path of continual change and experimentation:

- One of the first colleges to include adult learning in its charter
- The first to develop a low-residency model for higher education, and
- The first to offer residential programs for single parents receiving public assistance.[4]

Tim Pitkin and the reborn Goddard soldiered forward, through good years and lean, until an American educational landscape without their presence became all but unthinkable. The new college's life-changing transition developed an enduring appeal to an unorthodox group of students seeking an alternative education, thanks in large part to the personal magnetism of Tim Pitkin and his remarkable faculty. If Goddard seemed more than a little quirky to some observers, it was pure dogma to others. Goddard had graduated its first class in 1943, and one of the first two graduates was Evalyn Bates, Pitkin's secretary and a onetime Seminary student. She would later return to Goddard as Pitkin's special assistant and, eventually, the school's director of adult education.

The new Goddard remained experimental and progressive, if unaccredited and small for its first twenty-one years of operation. But Pitkin's unflagging efforts for uniform acceptance finally paid off in 1959: Goddard College received accreditation. In its first two decades, Goddard had built a reputation as one of the country's great innovators. The school used discussion as the basic method in classroom teaching, while accommodating the round-the-clock lives of students in determining personal curricula and practical work. The college itself had developed into a self-governing learning community in which everyone had a voice.

Tim Pitkin's personal star had also been rising. Both in education circles and beyond, Pitkin had simultaneously become a figure of both quiet renown and enduring respect in Vermont and the nation at large. He had received honorary degrees from a host of admiring institutions—many of which owed much to his outsized influence, including such colleges as

Nasson, Hartwick, and Windham—as well as the University of Vermont. In his spare time, Pitkin served a number of worthy extracurricular causes: as president of the Vermont and Quebec Universalist-Unitarian Convention; chairman of the section on residential adult education of the Adult Education Association; president of the Vermont Foundation of Independent Colleges; member of the board of directors for the Advancement of Small Colleges; and as Chairman of the Committee on Research and Development of the Council for the Advancement of Small Colleges. Additionally, during World War II, he was a public panel member of the War Labor Board before serving as an arbitrator in labor-management disputes.

But tiny Goddard remained the center of his world, both personally and philosophically. After 1959, Tim Pitkin set his sights on the second phase of his dream: spreading the college's wings. Pitkin's copilot in this new venture was Evalyn Bates, now his special assistant and instigator of a daring plan for Goddard. Having been an adult student at the college herself—Bates had once titled her Goddard senior study assignment "Two Projects in American Education"—Bates had been experimenting with adult education issues for years, both in the United States and abroad. Having been a Fulbright Scholar in Australia, working under the University of New England after earning her master's degree in 1957 from the University of Chicago, she was eager to push Goddard forward as an example of progressive education that works for adults. Evalyn Bates herself reminisced a half-century later about her interaction with Pitkin over this plan.[5]

"My recollection is that it took some prodding for him [Pitkin] to think about it," she told an interviewer in 2007. "He wasn't too keen on the idea at first; he didn't understand its dimensions." But Bates argued that in attracting mature students, "you have to design a program for them. You have to have a program that meets their needs and allows them to have space for learning."[6]

In 1963, Pitkin accepted the Bates plan—he had not been enthusiastic about a program for adult, nonresidential students when she first proposed it, although her persistence had eventually won him over. Now it would emerge fully formed, much like Athena bursting from the forehead of Zeus. It would establish the country's first low-residency college program for those unable to move to Goddard's campus—giving a radical new meaning to the term "off-campus student"—and thereby set in motion a model that would reverberate into the next century as the early standard for distance education and online courses of decades yet to come. Goddard's Adult Degree Program would be Pitkin's most lasting legacy, in one respect, as the only part of Goddard's program to survive into the twenty-first century.[7]

Pitkin could hardly have known that the joint venture he now planned—the voluntary consortium of willing colleges and universities with values similar to those he had long preached through Goddard—would become perhaps his broadest legacy of innovation beyond Goddard. Nor could he know just how much of his time this new plan would require over the next decade, whether as inspiration, as facilitator, or as spiritual guide.

And as first chairman of the board of the new Union for Research and Experimentation in Higher Education, Pitkin would soon find himself in for perhaps the most exhilarating ride of his long and unconventional life.

*"We intend this to be an action-oriented group…"* [8]

## Chapter 1: The Union is Born

Tim Pitkin's dream of a far-reaching "union" of progressive schools began to gestate seriously in early 1963, when he made plans to hold a special winter conference at Goddard to discuss the impact of the future of the experimental college in America."[9] One of a number of anniversary conferences in Plainfield, this conference held perhaps the highest priority for Pitkin. He was still not sure just how far the Goddard sphere of influence extended—years later, he saw it as more influential on conventional colleges than on other experimenting schools—but Pitkin was feeling adventuresome.

At the persistent urging of aide Evalyn Bates, Pitkin finally implemented her long-favored plan to create an Adult Degree Program at Goddard that year. "I think Goddard was one of the few places that took seriously the idea that adult college students could make their own minds up about what they wanted to do," Bates recalled in 2007, and quickly credited her boss with "actually making it happen" at Goddard."[10] Whether other colleges would emulate the plan was anyone's guess, but Pitkin forged ahead, never shy about publicizing his school's latest innovation.

The presidents and other executives of at least eight colleges—all members of the Conference of Experimental Colleges—responded to his call. Some were already associated with Goddard, but others were less familiar to Pitkin, who was more aware of experimentation going on at the campuses of some participants, most notably at Antioch College in Yellow Springs, Ohio; the new Monteith College of Wayne State University in Detroit, Michigan; and Sarah Lawrence College in Bronxville, New York. Still, he was pleased to involve any interested school in this serious attempt at brainstorming at the March conference titled "The Impact and Future Role of the Experimenting College."

This conference was "the first time administrators from a large number of experimental schools met as a group to talk about the history, influence, program, and role of this kind of college," according to a later chronicler of the event.[11] In attendance were presidents, vice presidents, and deans from Antioch, Goddard, Monteith, and Sarah Lawrence; Bard College in Annandale-on-Hudson, New York; and New College of Hofstra University, Hempstead, Long Island. Newcomers to the Goddard circle included Stephens College of Columbia, Missouri, and Reed College of Portland, Oregon. Observer schools at the conference included Chicago Teachers College North of Chicago, Illinois; Florida Atlantic University of Boca Raton, Florida; Nasson College in Springvale, Maine; and the State Colleges of New Jersey.[12]

But the mood at the conference in Plainfield, much like the New England weather in late March, was neither optimistic nor especially encouraging, at least at first. "With the snow two feet deep and the temperature fifteen below zero, top administrators from a dozen colleges converged on Goddard to share gloomy speculations," according to *Newsweek*'s account, published a week later.[13] President William Fels of Vermont's Bennington College, perhaps one of the best-known presenters, sketched the duties set for him by his college's graduates: "To see that Bennington does not change in any respect—and to see that it remains an experimental college." Bill Fels later reiterated the dilemma faced by his fellow experimenters: "Aren't the big bad colleges the really experimental ones now?" he wondered aloud. "Are the classic experimental colleges now conservative forces?"[14] This question troubled the leading administrators of the schools in the audience as well.

If none of the schools was interested in becoming either "big" or "bad," least of all Goddard or Pitkin, all were determined to remain experimental, and all seemed eager to take something concrete away from this conference.

Pitkin was aware that brainstorming was valuable in getting an experiment going. But he hoped for far more than talk from this group. "We took a look at what had happened and what was happening in experimental colleges, and what might happen in the future," Pitkin recalled in 1975.[15] Among the featured speakers was G. Kerry Smith, executive director of the Association for Higher Education of the National Educational Association, who "spoke to the need for a study of the national impact of experimental colleges," almost certainly as music to Pitkin's ears.

Monteith's Woodburn Ross quickly proposed the course of action Pitkin had been eagerly hoping for: "to set up a committee to determine ways of continuing this exchange among experimental colleges."[16] The group then selected an organizing committee, consisting of Pitkin and three other presidents: William Fels of Bennington, James P. Dixon of Antioch, and Paul L. Ward of Sarah Lawrence.[17]

The committee members met the following month to begin building the as-yet-undefined organization, later described as one "which would work with member colleges to support the interchange of ideas and the role of experimental colleges, and to help them have greater impact in America."[18] Of necessity, the schools signing on would have to be a kind of "clubby group," at least at first, with similar aims and interests, so Pitkin thought.[19] But the clear hope was to expand this core as quickly as possible, without sacrificing momentum or structural integrity.

By the time the committee met again in January of 1964 to ratify articles of incorporation, Pitkin and his fellow organizers had realized that someone else would be needed at the helm—a part-time leader at first, becoming full-time as soon as revenue permitted. Such a job would require the talents of a versatile executive officer, someone with experience in administering experimental programs, and someone with a sense of adventure, who was willing to take a risk. Not surprisingly, not everyone they approached was interested in such a nebulous task.

California college administrator Ernest L. Boyer was among the first to be sounded out. While Ernie Boyer was "intrigued by the union concept," Pitkin recalled, "he was a little scared of the funding problem," and unsure of working with so many different schools at once.[20] Boyer had already chaired a 1963 anniversary conference at Goddard—on

"Education and the Behavioral Sciences"—and was committed to innovation. But he soon backed away from the job offer at the new Union; a year later, he would instead become the first executive dean of the State University of New York (SUNY)—with more than fifty campuses—and in 1970, he would go on to become that state university system's chancellor.

Still, Boyer retained fondness for the Union idea. One of his early SUNY creations, the off-campus Empire State College at Saratoga Springs—modeled on the Goddard Adult Degree Program (ADP)—would later become a full member of the new Union, under the man who eventually accepted Pitkin's offer: Sam Baskin, director of program development and research in education at Antioch.

The eventual choice of Sam Baskin was both inspired and a bit problematic, if only for larger reasons of image, experience, and prominence. A graduate of New York University's School of Education, Baskin was a respected figure at Antioch in Yellow Springs, Ohio, where he was also professor of guidance and psychology, and hailed by Union leaders as a "nationally recognized leader in experimentation and research in higher education."[21] If fairly young—just forty-three years old at the time—and with experience limited to two small colleges, Antioch and Stephens, he was energetic and brilliant, and a protégé of movers and shakers at NYU; he had also served as a consultant for academic planning and program development at a number of colleges and universities.

But because he would also still work for Antioch, the image of the new Union was likely to be associated in many minds from the outset with the Yellow Springs campus, where the new Union would be headquartered.[22] As a part-time president, Baskin would also have to wear two hats—both Antioch's and that of the new Union's president, for the first two years. While Pitkin was not concerned with this dual role that blurred the lines, he did admit there were "some who felt it wasn't right for Antioch to get the credit for an idea which originated at Goddard"[23]—even if other observers believed Antioch actually deserved about as much credit as Goddard did for the group's efforts. It seemed that in the world of progressive education and experimentation, egos and personal feelings still mattered.

Most of those who had signed on at the 1963 conference remained deeply interested and involved, despite initial misgivings. But by the time Baskin's appointment was ready to be unveiled in February 1965, at the first annual conference, the new Union for Research and Experimentation in Higher Education—complete with its unwieldy name and list of founding members—the roster of interested parties had begun to shift slightly.[24] Two schools had dropped out: Bennington, after the sudden death of Bill Fels in November 1964, and Reed College, which apparently chose not to join for unknown reasons. But one newcomer signed up after hearing about the Union plans: tiny Shimer College in Mount Carroll, Illinois, whose innovative credentials included an early entrant program, in place since 1950, for students who had not yet completed high school. And other schools were waiting in the wings.

The board of the new Union for Research and Experimentation in Higher Education—compressed into an inelegant and nearly unpronounceable acronym, UREHE—would be chaired, not surprisingly, by Tim Pitkin. Joining him on that first board were fellow organizers James Dixon of Antioch and Paul Ward of Sarah Lawrence; Dean Woodburn Ross of Monteith, Dean Jerome Sachs of Chicago Teachers College North, and New College director Adolph G. Anderson; and four presidents: Reamer Kline of Bard, Roger C. Gay of Nasson, F. J. Mullin of Shimer, and Seymour Smith of Stephens.[25]

The total enrollment of the ten colleges represented on the UREHE board was just over 11,000 students—smaller than many single colleges in the Northeast—and presumably not enough to throw much weight around the educational landscape jointly, let alone individually. Yet the combined influence of the participant schools tended to belie their small size, as did their stated mission. And while the schools of UREHE might be considered by many observers as just removed from the mainstream of U.S. higher education, no one underestimated their effectiveness in setting trends or clearing a path of innovation through the thicket of sameness practiced by larger, more traditional institutions.

According to the Union's first official press release, issued by Goddard, the Union was being formed for three reasons:[26]

| 1 | To foster cooperative efforts in experimentation and research among the member colleges; |
|---|---|
| 2 | To encourage experimentation and research by faculty members within the member colleges themselves; and |
| 3 | To disseminate information regarding the Union's activities through conferences and publications. |

But there was one important caveat that Pitkin buried on the second page of that release: "The Union chooses not to be bound by any rigid definition of experiment and research." This almost cryptic assertion was followed by the expressed "hope to improve educational practices at colleges everywhere, not just among Union members."[27] The shadow of John Dewey still loomed large over the uncharted landscape, and the possibilities, if not endless, were more than a little intriguing.

Among the possibilities discussed was a plan to begin drawing up specific proposals for founding member Nasson College, one "that might be helpful to it in establishing its experimental campus."[28] Founded as a two-year college for women in 1912, Nasson was still struggling to find a competitive identity when it joined the new Union. Its Springvale campus had become a four-year college in 1935, had admitted men in 1952, and was fully accredited, but it was not growing as fast as President Roger Gay and others associated with Nasson would have wanted.

In 1963, Roger Gay had first proposed the "possibility of having one or more colleges under the control of Nasson College." According to the school's history, "the aim was to provide a liberal education involving extensive student participation in social, academia, and discipline policy" as well as education relying on "independent study in provinces of knowledge" and "not in individual courses."[29] This kind of language seemed to channel Tim Pitkin, noted for speaking large, pushing the envelope as far as it would go, and determinedly nurturing innovation wherever he could find it. A successfully reinvented Nasson would be the first example, Pitkin hoped, of a rising wave of experimentation among smaller colleges, led by the collective wisdom and hard experience of those forerunners who had exemplified the best practices in experimentation for decades.

In Chairman Giles's words, the conference participants would be charged with deciding precisely what to create "if you were offered the chance to set up this new college at Nasson." And at the same time, they needed to conceptualize "the most needed kind of college educational enterprise in America today."[30] The discussions at the February conference had gone on for many hours, building the kind of lasting bonds many at Goddard had hoped for and discovering the true depths of the schools' shared values and concerns.

Those schools actually joining the new Union would have to swallow hard and pay for the privilege of exerting a group influence. The membership fee of $3,500 per school, annually, represented more than a year's tuition for a student at Goddard or the other schools. If not a prohibitive sum, the $3,500 was a mildly uncomfortable line item for some in an era of limited budgets, but most of the founders, at least, were now firmly committed to the cost. An annual budget of $35,000 among the ten schools, however, could be stretched only so far; the Union's small core membership could not realistically finance the ambitious programs that were already being floated as possibilities. To put all of its programs on a stable footing, the Union's first and most pressing goal was to attract more members, enough to make the budget more substantial and its dreams—including hiring a full-time president—more credible as soon as practical. For the time being, much of the burden for achieving this quick growth would now fall on the capable shoulders of Sam Baskin.

Despite never having been a college president himself, Baskin now presided over a union of school composed, for all practical purposes, of just ten college leaders: seven presidents, including his own boss, two deans, and one director. And these ten were a varied lot, with a wide range of philosophies joined by a love of innovation and seasoned by hard-won experience.

Of the seven college presidents, those of Goddard (Pitkin) and Antioch (Dixon)—long regarded as leaders in the world of experimental higher education—essentially represented different ends of the experimental spectrum. The perspectives of their companions on the board fell somewhere in between. And some could point to lack of years in leadership positions as problematic, only one—Dr. Roger Crowell Gay, a Harvard graduate and leader of Nasson since 1950—had been at his school for much more than a decade; most were recent appointees, having served for five years or less. But no one could fault the Union leaders' initiative, resourcefulness, and enterprise. Dr. Francis J. ("Joe") Mullin, a biologist by training, had weathered critical financial crises at tiny Shimer since 1954 by seeking to build "a community of scholars where intellectual inquiry is the highest value."[31] Dr. Reamer Kline, an Episcopal priest who also taught Hebrew and the humanities arrived at Bard in 1960 as the unexpected savior of a school its board was on the verge of liquidating.[32] At Stephens since 1958, Dr. Seymour Smith had already helped turn the women's junior college into a four-year school but was newly struggling to distinguish itself from its competitors in a world rapidly changing over to coed institutions.[33]

Among the non-presidents of schools comprising the UREHE's board were Dr. Woodburn O. Ross (Monteith in Detroit, Michigan); Dr. Jerome M. Sachs (Northeastern Illinois University); Dr. Adolph G. Anderson (Hartwick College in Cooperstown, New York); and Dr. Paul Ward (Sarah Lawrence). Dr. Ross, dean of the fledgling Monteith College, had been an English professor at Wayne State when the experimental Monteith was born in 1959. Dr. Sachs and Dr. Anderson would become presidents of their respective schools by the end of the decade. Mathematician Sachs, appointed the first dean of Chicago Teachers-North in 1962, would remain there as its first president in 1966.[34] Anderson, director of Hofstra's New College, was a respected chemistry professor and accomplished singer; after becoming president of Hartwick College in 1969, he would help his new school "develop a more flexible and innovative curriculum and remain in close contact with the new Union."[35]

Last, but not least, was Dr. Paul Ward, head of Sarah Lawrence since 1960, a noted historian with a PhD from Harvard, and the new Union's first secretary; ironically, he would be the earliest to leave the board, to become head of the American Historical Association, later in 1965.[36] Ward's sudden departure presaged, perhaps, the departure of Sarah Lawrence from the Union, followed rather quickly by that of Nasson; both schools would be gone from the Union by the end of 1969, replaced by more adventurous schools from other parts of the nation.

"We intend this to be an action-oriented group," Baskin declared in the initial press release about Union. "We mean to ask ourselves some hard questions about our present practices in teaching and learning, to test out new ideas and new ways of accomplishing our purposes, and to accompany this experimentation with research and evaluation."[37]

Much of the responsibility for the Union's new work, Baskin pointed out, would be given to the individual faculties of the member schools. "Union members intend to give their faculties the opportunity to propose experiments and studies for consideration," Baskin noted, and he directed an active course ahead: "The stress will be as much on experimentation and exploration as on research and evaluation of the effects of change."[38]

The prospect of managing the founding members' widely varying expectations—and the iconoclastic temperaments and personalities of the leaders of these schools—required much patience, understanding, and wisdom, as well as a sense of humor. All these attributes Sam Baskin seemed to possess in abundance. Furthermore, Sam Baskin had a strong sense of purpose and a critical eye. He would need these many significant qualities, and more, as the great adventure began and the dream of the new Union began.

# FOUNDING PRESIDENT

## Samuel Baskin, PhD *(1921–2002)*

---

| THE UNION FOR RESEARCH AND EXPERIMENTATION IN HIGHER EDUCATION *(UREHE), 1965–1970* | PRESIDENT, THE UNION FOR EXPERIMENTING COLLEGES AND UNIVERSITIES *(UECU), 1970–1976* |
|---|---|

Sam Baskin's service to making the Union concept a reality began in February 1965, when he accepted a two-year, half-time appointment at the request of the board of trustees of a new higher-ed member consortium. What followed, in fact, was more than a decade of service to the Union for Research and Experimentation in Higher Education and its successors, during which time the Baskin name became synonymous with innovative trends in American higher education, and he became known as one of the nation's premier educators.

At the time of his appointment, Dr. Baskin was serving as a professor of psychology and as director of educational planning and development at Antioch College in Yellow Springs, Ohio, a founding member school of the fledgling Union experiment. A 1942 graduate of Brooklyn College with a bachelor's degree in psychology and pre-law, Baskin also held a master's degree in education (1948) and a PhD in guidance and personnel administration (1954) from New York University.

Baskin had been at Antioch since 1951, after having taught at both Stephens College of Columbia, Missouri, and at his alma mater, NYU. His lifelong mission was later described as "creating and developing alternative life study programs." During his pioneering presidency, the Union took on a new name—the Union for Experimenting Colleges and Universities (UECU), in 1970—and later, he oversaw the creation of both the freestanding Union Graduate School and the independent University Without Walls (UWW) program.

His philosophy drew nationwide attention when Fred Hechinger, education editor of *The New York Times*, penned a lengthy article (December 27, 1970) on the University Without Walls experiment, in which Baskin described the UWW as "an effort to develop new models and new forms for American higher education."

After Dr. Baskin resigned from the presidency of the UECU in 1976, he moved to Miami, Florida, where he remained active in the field of higher education. In 1977, he directed the Goodwin Watson Institute for Research and Development, a doctoral degree program under UECU auspices with special focus on institutional change, program development, and research in higher education. In his later years, Dr. Baskin served as a senior consultant for businesses and organizations such as University Consultants, Dayton Communication Corporation, and the Ford Foundation.

Baskin was the editor of *Organizing Non Traditional Study* (Jossey-Bass, 1974) and *Higher Education: Some Newer Developments* (McGraw-Hill, 1965), and the author of numerous articles and book chapters in educational scholarship. Among his many awards was the Distinguished Alumni Achievement Award from the NYU School of Education, presented to him in 1970.

The oldest son of Russian immigrants Benjamin and Rose Baskin, Sam Baskin was born on October 4, 1921, in Brooklyn, New York, where he grew up with two brothers, Arnold and Alex. His father was a carpenter. Dr. Baskin's death came in 2002, during his recuperation from injuries received in an automobile accident, according to his obituary in *The New York Times* (May 23, 2002). *The Times* listed his survivors as his wife, Florence; two sons, Robert and David; and three grandchildren.

In July 2002, the Union Institute & University Board of Trustees paid the following tribute to Dr. Baskin:

"Nearly 40 years ago, the great teachers and courageous minds who founded this university chose Dr. Samuel Baskin to lead the national consortium in exploring ways to broaden and expand American higher education. Under Dr. Baskin's leadership, this historic consortium challenged the structures of traditional higher education and dared to devise exemplary alternative paths to learning."[39]

*". . . to place our bets on the far edge of what seems possible"* [40]

## CHAPTER 2: THE BASKIN ERA

In the early spring of 1965, Sam Baskin prepared to assume the reins of Union, a hybrid organism with no precedent in American educational history. Much like the fabled three blind men determining what kind of animal an elephant was by feeling different parts of its body—and reaching wildly different conclusions—the ten founding schools could only bring differing, perhaps complementary, expectations to the experimental union they had created.

More immediately relevant to Baskin, however, was the underlying tension in his complicated chain of command. He had two bosses: his own president at Antioch, James Dixon, and the chair of his Union board of trustees and president of Goddard, Tim Pitkin. While both men shared farsighted views of the need for innovation in higher education, each offered a competing strategy, as exemplified in the traditions and histories of their individual schools.

Goddard and Antioch, separated by 800 miles on the map and different founding traditions, had faced difficult financial situations more than once since the mid-nineteenth century; both had been forced to reinvent themselves on occasion to survive. Antioch had begun as a full-college venture of the breakaway Christian Connection movement in 1850; Goddard had grown from a high school seminary operated by Unitarian-Universalists into a four-year college more recently, under Pitkin. By this time, the schools now seemed relatively stable, and willing to work from their respective strengths.

Both schools shared an appreciation for cooperative education, long a mainstay at Antioch and practiced in an in-house fashion at Goddard. Perhaps more than at other member schools, Pitkin's faculty at Goddard was excited by the prospect of closer associations with other experimental colleges in what would become Baskin's Union for Experimenting Colleges and Universities (UECU), having lost touch with what was occurring at Bard, Bennington, and Sarah Lawrence, with whom they had once had strong ongoing contacts. The Goddard faculty, like their leader, had felt somewhat isolated from experimentation at other schools, and had once hoped to learn much from interaction with Sarah Lawrence and Bennington.

But the gospels of independent study were at variance between Pitkin's Goddard and Dixon's Antioch. Goddard took a purist's view of the concept. Real independent study, in Pitkin's phrasing, "requires the student to come up with his own program," and not simply to follow an instructor's syllabus and overall plan, as Antioch allowed. To Pitkin, Antioch's practice was "really just individualized study."[41] Goddard had tried "individualized study" once, when "there weren't enough students to make up a class," but had long since moved on. What Antioch had become very good at in recent years, Pitkin thought, was "capitalizing on ideas."[42]

Meanwhile, Dixon, a physician who had been at Antioch only since 1959, had already achieved a national presence for his small school and his course of independent study. He and his faculty had obtained grant funding for Antioch's project emphasizing independent study at the same time Goddard was working out its own rather different, more innovative version. Pitkin believed Antioch had stopped its "real experimenting" in the 1920s, when the legendary Arthur Morgan had revamped the entire curriculum.

Still, whatever competition existed between Goddard and Antioch, or their current leaders, was more the result of a friendly philosophical divide than anything else. Antioch, perhaps, calculated its risks more pragmatically—and in so doing, got more credit in the public mind for its efforts than Goddard, accredited only since 1959. The rival terms, terminology and leadership would require much of Baskin's skill.

Another factor threatening consensus of the Union board was the political landscape of the 1960s. Yellow Springs and its campus were also fast becoming a hotbed of vocal, progressive political opinions—both among its students and the broader community—and Antioch seemed willing to endure notoriety for social views that many Americans would have considered extreme, especially on the issues civil rights and the Vietnam War. King Cheek, one later leader of Union who spent time in Yellow Springs, saw it as a cauldron of change, with both promise and obstacles: "The Antioch I knew was always in a state of continuous revolution," Cheek recalled in 2014. "And I believe change is wonderful … but only if you know where you want to take the change."[43]

To some observers, Antioch did not know precisely where its change was headed. If such progressive activism would later go hand in hand with the modern college experience on many far larger campuses, it seemed magnified first on the campuses of small schools such as Antioch, to which freethinking students seemed to gravitate more and more.

Since Dr. Reamer Kline, president of Bard since 1960, was one of the Union's board leaders, his school offered a third perspective, perhaps: innovation and stability, combining tradition with experimentation. Founded in 1860 as Saint Stephen's College and renamed for its founder in 1934, Bard had nearly closed—a cautionary tale of good intentions that had very nearly collapsed amid financial troubles and internal strife less than a decade earlier—before Reamer Kline's steady hand and surprisingly effective stewardship restored it to stability. In a little more than four years on the job, the former parish priest had won over skeptical students and rebellious faculty alike. Kline's success in stabilizing Bard had come, in part, by restoring the independent school's links to the Episcopal Church, but without sacrificing the progressive atmosphere and academic excellence, which had long distinguished the small school.[44]

Few experimental colleges saw the need to enforce conformity among students, which ran counter to the concept of experimentation itself. As the idea of experimental education began to spread to larger campuses in the 1960s, the infectious freewheeling atmosphere of smaller colleges would follow, breathing fresh air into the often moribund uniformity of larger schools—or at least, that seemed to be the hope of Pitkin, Dixon,

Kline, and many on the board of the new Union. Baskin's task would be to referee the inevitable disagreements among the strong-minded board members—even as the cast of distinguished members changed over the years—and help them design productive experiments that would also appeal to other schools.

Pitkin would be further disappointed by Nasson's departure, which felt it wasn't getting its money's worth; the new Union had clearly hoped to use Nasson as a public test case of the worth of its joint efforts.[45]

But even with the loss of Ward and the imminent loss of two of its founding schools, the Union began to gain ground almost immediately, with two new members signing on by the end of 1966: New College of Sarasota, Florida, and Loretto Heights College of Denver, Colorado. Sam Baskin's deft touch, particularly in responding to the board's thoughts and directives, helped ease the way for growth and stability as the new Union forged ahead. He would recall the Pitkin era—which came to an end in 1969, when Pitkin retired from the Goddard presidency—with a mixture of admiration and understated relief:

"I take many lessons away from my association with Tim. Not the least are lessons in courage," Baskin said in a 1969 interview. "He speaks his mind and can be tough and discomforting, but always in the belief that our task is to free the spirit and place our bets on the far edge of what seems possible… I have learned from Tim that the degree to which we feel we have come out with just solutions will depend on whether we dare, as Tim dared, to stand up for what we believe."[46]

## Baskin's Initiatives

Beginning in 1965, Baskin began marshaling the energies of the board and the faculties of the members for a concerted effort toward that "far edge of what seems possible." Among the many initiatives he helped produce, at least three deserve special note for their historical significance to the Union: 1) Project Changeover; 2) the University without Walls (UWW); and 3) the Union Graduate School (UGS).

### 1. Project Changeover

Project Changeover, the first major initiative of the UREHE era, used a grant of $288,592 from the Charles F. Kettering Foundation—announced in late 1966—to set up a three-year program for training faculty members, primarily from Union member schools. The stated purpose of the project was "to assist college faculty members in developing and trying out new methods of teaching," according to a 1984 UECU report.[47] Nearly one hundred faculty members—mostly from Union schools but also representing non-Union schools, attended the four-week summer sessions, held at Stephens College in 1967, Nasson College in 1968, and New College (Sarasota) in 1969, including follow-up sessions after a year of "experimental" teaching on home campuses.[48]

New College, in fact, appears to have been drawn into the fold largely by Project Changeover, touted in a news release announcing New College's entry into the Union: "Under Project Changeover, selected college faculty members are aided in developing creative changes in their classroom work through participation in an instructional summer workshop followed by trial periods in the classroom. Successes of the program are then made available through publication of the results."[49] The Kettering Foundation, founded in 1927, had recently progressed from giving grants to work-study programs at colleges to a broader, experimental phase by the 1960s. According to its own description, major projects funded that decade included the Institute for Development of Educational Activities, Inc. (I/D/E/A), "which worked to use the latest theories of primary and secondary education to change the way children were taught" and the Dartmouth Conferences, a series of cross-cultural forums involving prominent US and Soviet citizens. By the 1970s, Kettering's trustees would shift focus again, this time into a new phase: conducting its own research.[50]

Much like that Kettering shift, the Union's focus was evolving as well, after its small but impressive start with Project Changeover. By 1970, its success on a limited scale had inspired Baskin and the board of trustees of the now-renamed Union for Experimenting Colleges and Universities (UECU) to try for something larger, this one outside the traditional setting. If the ivy-covered walls of traditional closed campuses were more limiting than helpful in expanding experimentation by adventurous students, why have the walls at all?

## 2. University Without Walls (UWW)

Other schools had doubtless considered such an idea but discarded it for practical reasons—whether due to institutional resistance, general skepticism, lack of external funding, or other factors—but at least one foundation with deep pockets viewed the concept of a university without walls as a goal worth pursuing: the legendary Ford Foundation, among the world's largest philanthropic organizations. Founded in 1936 by automobile tycoon Henry Ford, the Foundation had devoted itself to a wide range of imaginative projects in the three decades since. Still governed at this time in the 1960s by a Ford family member—Ford's grandson Henry Ford II—the philanthropic organization emphasized education as one of its five major goals, especially in its effort to "promote greater equality of educational opportunity" and "enable individuals to realize more fully their ... potential."[51]

The creative environment of the 1960s made almost any dream seem possible, and the Ford Foundation's amenability to innovative projects made it a natural sounding board for fresh, original ideas in education. It was therefore hardly surprising that a proposal to create a university without walls would be floated before Ford Foundation leaders by the late 1960s. What *was* surprising was that two very similar proposals—independent in origin—would appear within a short period of time, and that Ford leaders suggested that the creators join forces.

One of those proposals came from Sam Baskin and Union. But it echoed an ironically similar proposal from King Cheek, who then was serving as president of Shaw University in Raleigh, North Carolina, a private, historically black college founded just after the end of the Civil War. And the coincidence—a happy one, in many ways—eventually brought Cheek into the Union family, just as Sam Baskin was beginning to feel the need to augment limited staff and look for a successor.

"Before the University Without Walls was started, I had the idea, independently of the Union, and I had already begun a conversation with the Ford Foundation about the concept," Cheek recalled four decades later. "Sam Baskin later went to the Ford Foundation about the same concept, and the people at Ford told him he should talk to me, because I had already been talking to them about it."[52]

Cheek had served Shaw as dean and vice president, and since 1969, as president. A graduate of Bates College, a Maine institution well regarded for its own tradition of innovation, he held both master's and law degrees from the University of Chicago.[53] His proposal for a university without walls, certainly a bold move for the tiny Shaw campus, heralded a promising future for students of all races by offering them an opportunity to advance their education without attending classes in a traditional setting. His relationship with Baskin, catalyzed by their Ford proposals, would gradually blossom into his appointment as UECU's first vice president in 1974, after a stint as president of Morgan State College. Cheek would also become a champion of the Union's longstanding efforts to assist historically black colleges and universities, known as HBCUs.

As the Union's University Without Walls eventually emerged, it was billed more as a "utopian university," largely the brainchild of a faculty group disappointed with Project Changeover's limited accomplishments.[54] According to an article in *Science Magazine,* it was designed for students from age sixteen to sixty and older, with an estimated annual tuition of $2,650. As crystallized in a cogent proposal[55] by Baskin and UECU director of research Edwin F. Hallenbeck—vice president of Roger Williams College, a new UECU member—the eight ideas central to the UWW sounded at once both familiar and somehow quite new[56]:

1. Inclusion of a broad range of persons, as many beyond the usual age for college would like to have and would profit from a college education. Many of them have acquired much skill and knowledge from their life experiences, which can and should be recognized as contributing to college level work and the degree.
2. Involvement of students, faculty members, and administrators in the design and development of each UWW unit. It is clear that students are less resistant to programs they themselves have helped to devise and operate.
3. Development of special seminars and other procedures to prepare students to learn on their own and . . . to prepare faculty members for the new instructional procedures to be used in the UWW program.
4. Employment of flexible time units, as no two students are exactly alike in their background, educational aptitudes, interests and needs. Programs were to be individually tailored by student and advisor. There would be no fixed curriculum and no uniform time schedule for the award of the degree.
5. Use of a broad array of resources for teaching and learning, both in and out of the classroom, recognizing that students also learn from their own firsthand experiences.
6. Use of an adjunct faculty involving many persons outside the regular educational institution who can contribute significantly to students' undergraduate experience ... Any society should include among its educators its best artists, scientists, writers, musicians, dancers, physicians, lawyers, industrialists, financiers, and other specialists.
7. Opportunities for students to use the resources of other UWW units in the network ... In addition, learning may be greatly enhanced if a student can be part of the "mix" of more than one educational institution.
8. Traditional assessment procedures (time spent in classrooms, course credits, grades, achievement tests on prescribed subject matter) do not reveal enough about the individual's growth and development ... One crucial task of the UWW program will be to find new approaches to evaluation that will periodically appraise the individual's cognitive and affective learning for the student and his advisor.

Although the UWW proposal required time to develop fully, but once operational, it was very nearly an overnight success for the Union. It certainly struck a welcome chord with major benefactors: the Ford Foundation, which provided $400,000 in February 1971[57]; the US Office of Education, which granted Union a total of $415,000; and the Carnegie Corporation, which provided $175,000 in the UWW's later years. Fred Hechinger of *The New York Times* hailed it in a lengthy Sunday edition article in December 1970, offering the Union a rare moment in the national spotlight.[58] And perhaps even more significantly, the UWW project attracted a host of new members to the UECU, which had grown from ten to eighteen members in 1970, nearly doubling its annual revenues—at $4,000 annually, a tidy sum of $72,000 in operating funds—and spreading its influence around the country.

Meanwhile, the Union staff was growing too slowly to keep up with the demand of new programs. By mid-1972, the UECU staff had grown somewhat to "a staff of four plus two secretaries" crowded into a "relatively small, two-story frame house" on the Antioch campus, according to the UWW accrediting team. Staff duties varied: assisting UECU members "in developing project proposals and in funding them," as well as providing consultant service and coordinating "such joint Union activities as its Graduate School and UWW" in addition to providing research assistance.[59]

In early 1971, when the UWW project was formally unveiled, a total of nineteen institutions of higher learning were listed as participants in what *Science* magazine described as "a cradle to grave process uncircumscribed by time or space."[60] Most participants were already members of the

UECU: Antioch, Bard, Chicago State, Friends World, Goddard, Loretto Heights, Morgan State, Northeastern Illinois State, Roger Williams, Skidmore, Staten Island Community, and Stephens colleges; New College (Sarasota); and the state universities of Massachusetts, Minnesota, and South Carolina. Two additional schools listed as participants—Howard University and New York University—were not Union members, although a third school, Shaw University, did join the UECU by 1972.[61]

By 1972, at least twenty UWW affiliates were listed, many located in the shadows of large public universities, such as the University of California, Berkeley, and the University of Massachusetts, from which adjunct faculty were likely to be drawn.[62] At the height of UWW expansion in the mid-1970s, UECU itself listed as many as thirty-four schools that were operating UWW branches; another estimate placed the figure at fifty UWW branches.[63] Some, like Oklahoma's UWW Flaming Rainbow, went on to become independent, if short-lived, colleges; less successful branches either ceased to exist or were gradually folded back into area institutions.

According to an unpublished report by Rick Hendra and Ed Harris in 1973, most of the earliest UWW students were adults—forty percent older than thirty years of age, and five percent older than fifty. Its appeal to adults was clearly the strongest single legacy of the short-lived UWW movement. But like its sibling—the Union Graduate School—the UWW also held a strong attraction for women and minorities, with startling numbers on both counts in 1976: "Half of all UWW and UGS students were women, 55 percent were older than 23 years, 32 percent were black,

12 percent were Spanish speaking, 4 percent were Native American, and .6 percent were Asian."[64]

By 1972, when the North Central Association of Colleges and Secondary Schools (NCA)—founded in 1895, a prestigious membership organization for educational accreditation of colleges, universities, and schools in nineteen states—granted pre-accreditation to the UWW, the program was thriving, and despite its newness, well past the toddler stage and nearing adolescence. More than 3,000 students were enrolled in the program in its first year, and UECU officials expected 4,500 or more to enroll in the second year.[65] As Sam Baskin noted with no small satisfaction in Union's September news release that year, it was a "first" in higher education;

> ...where a consortium of institutions will award a degree in the name of the consortium, and where that degree has been approved for full correspondent status. "What is even perhaps even more important ... is that the Association's approval comes for a program that departs rather radically in its plan and approach to higher education from most programs of undergraduate education.[66]

As noted by that accrediting team, the UWW program was "reform-oriented ... and builds on what might be called counter-principles" (or the term used later in the team's report, "Articles of Faith") before listing ten key elements that each UWW unit was expected to honor. The team had evaluated results at eight of the twenty UWW units, and was generally positive, almost effusive, in its assessment: "UWW, in short, is a going enterprise and a very healthy development for American higher education," and the UWW's students "are excited, interested, learning, confident of themselves and their future."[67] However, there were certain issues the NCA noted that could not be ignored as the UWW program grew.

"The team had found no evidence that the Union itself has accepted responsibility for student performance" through either of the normal methods used by traditional institutions: concrete procedures or plans to develop them. Furthermore, the report stated that UWW offered little "for handling and accounting for financial resources; for regulating appointments, promotions, and perquisites of personnel; and for controlling the curriculum and nature of the academic program."[68]

The NCA report was not intended to criticize the UWW program, for indeed the Union was *not* expected to "function like traditional institutions. Far from it." The Union was a consortium, not a traditional school, and had to find its own "other ways to measure quality, to assure its continuity, and to control those who render educational services in its name." The UWW "is clearly doing what it set out to do," the examiners concluded. "And what it set out to do is no minor modification, no mere gimmickry. It is a basic departure, a brave experiment that deserves a fair trial and respect, an undertaking that may very well become a part of higher education throughout the country."[69]

What troubled the team, if only in passing, was that "to date, the Union has not taken these steps, though it appears to be aware of the issues involved."[70] There was still so much to be done, and as yet, no sign of how or when.

The UWW was a proud achievement for the Union, still in its own developmental stages. But for all the surface success of the early UWW movement, storm clouds lay ahead on the horizon. The program's rapid expansion and the complicated task of managing so many new entities—many serving disadvantaged populations who often needed significant financial assistance—called for intensive, efficient management by a seasoned staff and a firm eye on the bottom line. In mid-1972, the Union, for all its idealism and energy, still seemed only vaguely aware of the urgency of addressing such long-range needs fully and thoroughly.

## 3. The Union Graduate School (UGS)

The Union Graduate School had been discussed as early as 1967 by various faculty members at the then-UREHE member schools, and plans continued to be refined in subsequent meetings. In June 1969, "authorization for award of the (doctoral) degree by the Union as a Consortium was obtained ... through the Ohio State Department of Education." Preliminary contacts then began with representatives of the North Central Association "for the purpose of planning toward accreditation," according to a February 1970 memorandum.[71]

After the renamed Union for Experimenting Colleges and Universities (UECU) was chartered as a degree-granting institution in the state of Ohio in 1970, the Union received from the Ohio Board of Regents authority to grant both baccalaureate and doctoral degrees in May 1971. The UGS was established first, and was granted candidate for accreditation status by the North Central Association in 1972.[72]

A January 1970 mimeographed document in the Union's files announced that the first colloquia for the doctoral students would be held in the summer of that year. In that document, the Union Graduate School was hailed as an "unusual PhD program, especially adapted for persons who for a variety of reasons cannot make the best possible use of the usual PhD programs at American colleges and universities." By utilizing "highly individualized programs of learning and ... a much broader range of resources than normally available," the UGS program promised to stress "independent study, consultation with faculty, use of internships, development of special projects and programs, and use of faculties and facilities of Union colleges and universities." In an effort to distinguish itself from traditional graduate school fare, the UGS program promised to be "long on creativity and short on 'time-serving;' long on self-reliance and short on teacher authoritarianism," with a minimum residence of one year and a yearly tuition of $2,000.[73]

Despite "very low key ... publicity," news of the graduate program spread quickly throughout educational circles, especially in the UECU college communities. A longer memorandum in February 1970 from Roy Fairfield, coordinator of the UGS program, and UECU Associate Director Goodwin Watson—which attributed the unsigned mimeographed announcement to Sam Baskin—sketched examples, without names, of the sixty-nine UGS applicants thus far tallied, with hundreds more having inquired. According to this document, the twenty-six applicants who had been selected for admission included an education planner with computer expertise and a master's degree in modern languages; a published poet and former college English instructor; a dean at one of the UECU member schools; a Kenyan student and faculty member with a master's degree in sociology; and a former teacher of humanities and literature, now a program development associate at a Union college.[74]

The UGS development plan called for the provision of program centers on the campuses of Union colleges, beginning with Antioch and Loretto Heights in the summer of 1970, with five or six centers expected to have opened by 1972. The proposed UGS educational process for the enrolled student was fairly straightforward. Assisted by an advisor from his/her center staff, the student would select a major advisor from the field of interest, either at the UGS center's college faculty, another institution of higher learning, or an expert from the outside world. Adjunct faculty members would be paid out of the UGS budget. Tuition details were not included, but by 1975, UGS tuition remained at the level foreseen in Sam Baskin's original announcement: $700 per quarter.

The program quickly became a very popular one, and by 1974, more than 350 students were enrolled across the country, almost all through the UGS central office and its numerous centers. Among the many early graduates of the PhD program in the 1970s were such notable students as George A. Pruitt (PhD 1974), later president of Thomas Edison State College in New Jersey, and chairman of the Union board of trustees from 2001 to 2003; Maravene Loeschke (PhD 1975), later president of Mansfield University and Towson University; Charles W. Simmons (PhD 1978), founder and president of Sojourner-Douglass College; and Thomas Rosandich (PhD 1978), president and CEO of the United States Sports Academy.[75]

Along with the expansion of its programs under Sam Baskin, the membership of Union had expanded regularly since its opening days. Its first two new members, admitted in October 1967, were New College at Sarasota, Florida, and Loretto Heights College in Denver, Colorado, both small private schools dedicated to experimentation. New College, led by new president John Elmendorf, had opened just three years earlier; its innovative pass-fail curriculum was designed by educators "who believed in the power of the mind and wanted to free both students and faculty from the limits of lock-step curriculum and a focus on credit hours and a GPA." Loretto Heights, affiliated with the Roman Catholic Sisters of Loretto, had been a four-year college since 1918; new president Sister Patricia Jean Manion intended to develop a "comprehensive program of independent studies and may experiment with the college within the college idea," both of which reflected wider Union practices.[76]

Yet not all of the original ten members were satisfied, for reasons of their own, and by 1969, the Union had lost three of its founders: Nasson College, Sarah Lawrence College, and Shimer College, dropping that year's total membership briefly to nine. Still, the Union's membership quickly rebounded, doubling in size to eighteen by February 1970, when nine schools—out of twenty applicants—were announced as new members of the UECU. These new members were:

1. Chicago State College, Chicago, IL; Milton Byrd, president;
2. Friends World College, Westbury, NY; Morris R. Mitchell, president;
3. Roger Williams College, Bristol, RI; Ralph E. Gauvey, president;
4. Staten Island Community College, NY; William M. Birenbaum, president;
5. University of Massachusetts (School of Education), Amherst; Oswald Tippo, chancellor

6. University of Minnesota, Minneapolis; Malcolm Moos, president;
7. University of the Pacific, Stockton, CA; Dr. Robert Burns, president;
8. Westminster College, Fulton, MO; Robert L. D. Davidson, president; and
9. University of Wisconsin at Green Bay; Edward W. Weidner, chancellor.[77]

By mid-1972, seven more new members had joined the Union[78]:

1. Community College of Baltimore, MD; Harry Bard, president;
2. Florida International University, Miami; Charles Perry, president;
3. Franconia College, Franconia, NH; Leon Botstein, president;
4. Morgan State College, Baltimore, MD; Andrew Billingsley, president;
5. Pitzer College, Claremont, CA; Robert H. Atwell, president;
6. Shaw University, Raleigh, NC; J. Archie Hargraves, president; and
7. Skidmore College, Saratoga Springs, NY; Joseph C. Palamountain, Jr., president.

Between 1972 and 1974, the Union added seven members, making a net gain of six members by 1974, as follows:[79]

1. College of Racine, Racine, WI (until it closed in 1974); Dean Russel, acting president;
2. Johnston College (University of Redlands), Redlands, CA; Pressley McCoy, chancellor;
3. Kirkland College, Clinton, NY; Samuel F. Babbitt, president;
4. Universidad Boricua, New York, NY; Victor G. Alicea, chancellor;
5. University of Alabama (New College), Tuscaloosa; F. David Mathews, president;
6. University of South Carolina, Columbia; Thomas Jones, president; and
7. Webster College, Saint Louis, MO; Leigh Gerdine, president.

In June 1974, the Union announced the addition of six more new members all at once, including public universities from California and

Illinois; two community schools aimed at educating disadvantaged minorities in California and Texas; and, for the first time, two freestanding UWW affiliates.[80] The six new schools joining in 1974 were:

1. Governors State University, University Park, IL; Leo Goodman-Malamuth, president;
2. Hispanic International University, Houston, TX; Robert Navarro, chairperson;
3. University of California Extension, San Diego; Martin Chamberlain, dean;
4. Universidad de Campesinos Libres, Fresno, CA; Ysidro R. Macias, director;
5. UWW Berkeley, Berkeley, CA; Victor Acosta, co-director; and
6. UWW Flaming Rainbow, Stilwell, OK; David Hilligoss, founding director.

This brought the total membership to thirty-four schools, according to UECU's count. Not emphasized, however, was the dramatic shift in the Union's balance between public and private members from its beginnings in 1965. Only one of the ten founding schools had been a publicly funded institution (Chicago Teachers College-North, later Northeastern Illinois University). By 1974, about one-third of all UECU members—ten of the thirty-four member schools listed on the UECU letterhead—were public institutions, most of which were much larger in terms of enrollment numbers than the original small private schools which had created Union. The concept of educational experimentation had now entered the mainstream and there seemed to be no turning back.

# A Snapshot in Time: *The Union in 1975*

A report compiled in early 1975 provides a clear snapshot of the Union program during the closing days of Sam Baskin's presidency.[81] His staff of ten included King Cheek, his vice president; seven directors, including one who doubled as registrar; and two program associates.

Directors listed in the *UECU Update* of April 1975 included Lee Roy Black, in charge of correctional education programs and the Teacher Corps program; Walter A. Buchmann, developing programs; Henry Chitty, programs for Native American students; Edwin F. Hallenbeck, research (and accreditation officer); Reggie Jones, UWW minority group programs; Jerry Mandina, high school/college UWW; and Renate Muffler, finances (and the Union registrar). Program associates included Linnhe Moeller and Mark Rosenman.

**Five categories of relationships** were listed between the Union and its program units and member institutions (enrollments as of October 1974):

### 1

**Program Units Awarding
the UECU Doctorate Degree**
*(Integral to UECU, directly operated)*

Union Graduate School, Yellow Springs, OH
  John C. Pool, interim director
  Enrollment: 335

Program for Innovation in Elementary
and Secondary Education, UGS, Yellow Springs, OH
  Roy P. Fairfield, acting coordinator
  Enrollment: 20

Urban Regional Learning Center UGS,
Morgan State College, Baltimore, MD
  Argentine Craig, director
  Enrollment: 1

### 2

**Program Units Awarding the UECU/UWW
Baccalaureate Degree**
*(All sponsored by a host institution and Union member, financially independent of the Union)*

UWW/Flaming Rainbow University, Stilwell, OK
  Henry Chitty, director
  Enrollment: 76

UWW/Hispanic International University, Houston, TX
  Ted Grossman, director
  Enrollment: 18

UWW/Roger Williams College, Bristol, RI
  Robert Leaver, director
  Enrollment: 163

## 2 continued

UWW/Skidmore College, Saratoga Springs, NY
    Mark Gelber, director
    Enrollment: 157

UWW/Westminster College, New Wilmington, PA
    Gale Fuller, director
    Enrollment: 7

UWW/Universidad Boricua, New York, NY
    Victor G. Alicea, chancellor
    Enrollment: 60

UWW/Universidad de Campesinos Libres, Fresno, CA
    Ysidro R. Macias, director
    Enrollment: 21

## 3 Program Units Awarding the Host Institution Degrees *(UWW units programmatically and financially responsible to host institutions)*

UWW/University of Alabama (New), Tuscaloosa, AL
    Bernard Sloan, director
    Enrollment: 21

UWW/Antioch College/West, San Francisco, CA
    Joseph McFarland, dean
    Enrollment: 244

UWW/Antioch/Philadelphia, PA
    David Frisby, director
    Enrollment: 185

UWW/Bard College, Annandale-On-Hudson, NY
    Irma Brandeis, director
    Enrollment: 31

UWW/University of California, Berkeley
    Victor Acosta, co-director
    Enrollment: 239

**3** *continued*

UWW/Chicago State University, Chicago, IL
William Charland, director
Enrollment: 75

UWW/Florida International University, Miami, FL
Dabney G. Park, director
Enrollment: 145

UWW/Franconia College, Franconia, NH
Paul (Skip) Lau, director
Enrollment: 8

UWW/Friends World College, Huntington, NY
George H. Watson, moderator
Enrollment: 277

UWW/Goddard College, Plainfield, VT
Tony Pearce, director
Enrollment: 135

UWW/New College/Hofstra University, Long Island, NY
Howard Lord, coordinator
Enrollment: 40

UWW/Johnston College, Redlands, CA
E. K. Williams, director
Enrollment: 22

UWW/Loretto Heights College, Denver, CO
Elinor Greenberg, director
Enrollment: 133

UWW/University of Massachusetts Amherst, Hadley, MA
Edward J. Harris, director
Enrollment: 299 enrolled

UWW/University of Minnesota, Minneapolis, MN
Jeffrey Johnson, director
Enrollment: 195

UWW/Northeastern Illinois University, Chicago, IL
Kenneth W. Stetson, coordinator
Enrollment: 138

## 3 continued

UWW/University of the Pacific, Stockton, CA
  Alan L. Mikels, director
  Enrollment: 9

UWW/Shaw University, Raleigh, NC
  Abdul Elkordy, director
  Enrollment: 500

UWW/Stephens College, Columbia, MO
  James Waddell, director
  Enrollment: 56

UWW/University of Wisconsin, Green Bay, WI
  Carol Pollis, director
  Enrollment: 53

## 4

**UECU Member Institutions Without Active UWW Units** *(Not operating either undergraduate or graduate programs interrelated with the Union)*

Community College of Baltimore
University of California Extension, San Diego
Governors State University
Kirkland College
Pitzer College
Webster College

## 5

**Affiliated Program Unit Awarding Host Institution Degree** *(Not a Union member, but actively affiliated with UECU/UWW network)*

UWW/Howard University,
  Anita Hackney, director
  Enrollment: 167

In April 1976, Sam Baskin announced his plans to leave the Union presidency by year's end, after more than a decade at the helm. His designated successor was to be King V. Cheek, Jr., UECU's vice president for planning and program development since 1974.[82]

As Baskin then reminded the UECU board, he had originally agreed to take the position on a two-year leave arrangement from Antioch College, and those two years had expanded to twelve. In response to Baskin's announcement, UECU Board Chairman James Werntz publicly commended Baskin as the Union's "most important member" who had provided Union with "stunning accomplishments."[83]

Werntz went on to acknowledge that Baskin "has done as much as any man I know to fuel the recent movement for educational reform and has put the Union as close as any national organization at the center of creative and responsible development of higher education." During Baskin's tenure, the Union's annual budget had grown nearly tenfold: from $35,000 in 1965 to more than $3 million in 1976. Between 1969 and 1976, the Union had received outside funding totaling at least $2.5 million.[84]

Werntz, a University of Minnesota physicist who headed that school's Center for Educational Development, was the third board chair in the Baskin era, having succeeded Reamer Kline as the chair in 1975. And before Baskin left the presidency, he would work briefly under a fourth board chair, and another familiar face: his longtime boss at Antioch, Jim Dixon, now a consultant in education, administration, and public health, whose election was noted in the same press release.[85]

Although Baskin might have been moving away from Yellow Springs—the Antioch campus, where he had labored for twenty-five years—he was still far from leaving the Union behind. Instead, he was moving into the directorship of a new UECU project: the Goodwin Watson Institute for Research and Program Development, a doctoral program for student leaders in "creative research ... [who] may make important social contributions." The Institute's name honored the veteran educator Goodwin Watson, who was then retiring in 1976 after "a long and exceptionally distinguished career in educational innovation," including eight years with the Union.[86]

At the Goodwin Watson Institute, to be located in Miami, Florida, Baskin would continue to teach, as the recipient of the first Goodwin Watson Distinguished Professorship in Higher Education honor. "This position will enable me to serve in the kind of catalytic leadership and development role at which I believe I am best," Baskin said. "The Institute will help give life to many of the ideas we have long talked about."[87]

The next phase of the Union's existence would unleash new issues, producing three successive leaders in the next six years. Each would seek to resolve issues caused, in part, by the rapid success of the Union that Sam Baskin had helped to fashion and nurture tirelessly for a dozen years. The Union would meet increasing and unexpected turbulence as it tried to confront educational challenges in the declining decades of the twentieth century.

# King Virgil Cheek, Jr., JD

PRESIDENT, THE UNION FOR EXPERIMENTING
COLLEGES AND UNIVERSITIES
*(UECU), 1976–1978*

King Virgil Cheek, Jr., second president of the Union for Experimenting Colleges and Universities, succeeded Sam Baskin as UECU leader in 1976. He held that post until his resignation in 1978.

A 1959 graduate of Bates College in Lewiston, Maine, Cheek earned both a master's degree (1967) and a law degree (1969) from the University of Chicago. Active in the civil rights movement, he took part in the 1963 March on Washington. The following year, his older brother James—then serving as president of Shaw University, a historically black private school in Raleigh, North Carolina—recruited him to serve there as a college dean and then vice president. When James Cheek left to become president of Howard University, King Cheek was named Shaw's president in 1969.

After serving as president of another historically black school, Morgan State University in Baltimore, Maryland, from 1971 to 1974, Cheek was selected as vice president of the UECU, serving under Dr. Baskin until acceding to the presidency in 1976. He was succeeded as UECU president in 1978 by acting president Dr. Kenneth W. Rothe.

After leaving UECU in 1978, Dr. Cheek went on to pursue other interests, cofounding the Center for Leadership and Career Development in Washington, DC. In 1985, he joined the faculty and administration of the New York Institute of Technology, eventually becoming vice president of academic affairs, and where he remains a professor of social science. He also served as chancellor of the New York College of Health Professionals, from 2001 to 2003. He is the author of numerous articles and books, including *The Quadrasoul*, a quartet of novels that explore four dimensions of the human spirit.

A native of Weldon, North Carolina, King Cheek was one of five children born to Baptist minister King V. Cheek, and his schoolteacher mother, Lee Ella Williams Cheek, who became the state's first black female insurance broker. His older brother, James Cheek, died in 2010.

In an interview given to *The History Makers Series (The Root,* September 19, 2011), King Cheek recalled the childhood trauma of being tongue-tied and having congenital cataracts:

At age 12 I was a young child evangelist, and I could have remained in that sphere. That was fulfilling, even more so because I no longer had a speech impediment. But I gave it up because I became disenchanted with organized religion and what I perceived it to represent. In the latter years of elementary school, about sixth or seventh grade, I decided that I wanted to be a lawyer because I enjoyed the art of advocacy. Not going to college was never an option in my family."

"I learned on my own, and I took charge of my own development. I knew I was not abnormal or retarded. At a very early age I started developing my own agenda, deciding what I wanted to do with my life. School was very important in our family

*"Change is wonderful . . .
if you know where you want to take the change."*
~ King V. Cheek

## CHAPTER 3: THE INTERIM ERA OF KING V. CHEEK AND KENNETH W. ROTHE

King Cheek had been recruited at the Union by Sam Baskin for several purposes, the most important of which was to succeed Baskin when he retired as president in October 1976. At the time of Cheek's appointment as vice president 1974, Baskin had praised his colleague's skill set and broad educational experience, expressing "delight that King Cheek, who has long worked for the same goals as the Union, has agreed to bring his skills and experience to our efforts," adding that Cheek's presence "will add great thrust to the Union's leadership role in effecting change in American higher education".[88]

Years later, Cheek recalled being initially attracted to the Union "because the Union had a special mission. The Union was started with a vision, a purpose. I was recruited to it by Goodwin Watson in the 1960s and was associated with the Union from 1968 to 1978," he said, beginning in his days as vice president of Shaw University.[89]

While serving as the Union's vice president for program planning and development, Cheek was Baskin's second-in-command for the two years, from 1974 until Baskin's retirement announcement. By the spring of 1976, Baskin paved the way for Cheek to become Union's second president, a position that officially began on October 1, 1976. The two had developed a close working relationship, and clearly respected each other. Yet Cheek wasted little time in taking up the challenge of replacing the man many saw as the public face of the Union, or in finding a new home for the Union's headquarters.

"The first thing I did was move the Union out of Yellow Springs," Cheek recalled in 2014. "In my opinion, it had become too closely identified with Yellow Springs and the Antioch atmosphere. Antioch was always in a state of continuous revolution. Well, I believe change is wonderful…*if* you know where you want to take the change." [90]

It was a big if. By 1976, that "continuous state of revolution" had already succeeded in toppling Jim Dixon, Antioch's president, from the college's top job. Although this was an upheaval for Dixon at Antioch, he remained on Union's board—succeeding James Werntz as board chair that same year—until 1978, during Cheek's own tenure. If the Union was now to succeed in establishing its own identity, separate from Antioch's shadow—as well as encourage all member schools to participate on more of an equal basis—it would need to do so in a more congenial setting. The leadership hoped that the newly independent Union might be situated in an urban environment and thus more accessible to travelers.

Cincinnati—just seventy miles to the south of Yellow Springs—was a natural choice, with a major airport, access to a growing interstate highway system, and many urban amenities not available in former rural environs.[91] After a brief search, the Union leadership located a suitable building at 2331 Victory Parkway, a leased building in the city's East

Walnut Hills neighborhood, and moved into those offices on July 1, 1977. This facility would remain the Union's new home until mid-1979.

While Union's graduate school program (UGS) would remain for the time being in Yellow Springs, the University Without Walls (UWW) program centers in Ohio would now be headquartered in Cincinnati, Cleveland, Columbus, and Dayton. Especially useful for growth and interest in the UWW program, a *Cincinnati Post* article at the time announced the Union's move to Cincinnati and promoted UWW tuition and time investment. For Ohioans, tuition then amounted to $2,100 annually, with most students earning their degrees in eighteen to thirty months.)[92]

And Cheek had already begun initiating other changes, as part of eight "broad target goals" he announced in his first month in office, as follows:

1. Expanding and renewing the consortium;
2. Strengthening the UECU degree program and achieving accreditation;
3. Developing a sound fiscal structure and support system;
4. Establishing a base and agenda for new program development;
5. Creating a more visible national presence and improving the Union's effectiveness as an interactive network;
6. Strengthening the Union's capacity for institutional research and analysis;
7. Creating a stable and efficient and efficient administrative/governance system; and
8. Reaffirming and continuing the implementation of the Union's mission.[93]

Cheek's goal of diversifying and expanding the Union's base led to an early decision to begin admitting non-degree-granting institutions, accounting for three of the seven schools admitted to membership during his first year. The board of trustees had taken this unprecedented action in part to stem a downward slide in the number of Union members, which had declined to nineteen from its peak of thirty-four. Those schools joining in 1977 were therefore an eclectic lot, including Union's first two members from outside the continental United States, in Canada and Puerto Rico:

1. **Canadian School of Management/Northland Open University**
   North York, ON, Canada
   George Korey, president
2. **Edwin Gould Outdoor Education Centers, Brewster, NY**
   Samuel B. Ross, president
3. **Martin Center, Indianapolis, IN**
   Rev. Boniface Hardin, OSB, director
4. **Mercyhurst College, Erie, PA**
   Martin Shane, president
5. **Ohio Institute of Practical Politics, Cincinnati, OH**
   Bailey Turner, dean
6. **Social Policy, New York, NY**
   Alan Gartner, president
7. **World University, San Juan, PR**
   Ronald C. Bauer, president

But even this temporary upsurge to twenty-six members was an aberration; by the end of 1978, membership would be cut in half, decreasing to a dismal thirteen. By this time, there were many factors accounting for the reduction of members—including the negative publicity surrounding the Union's forced bankruptcy in 1978—but even before this, competition for student enrollment among educational institutions in higher education remained a significant one. Nationwide, as other schools and Union's own member schools began to experiment independently, the need for the Union guidance was less obvious. At $4,000 a year, the UECU dues payments were scrutinized with increasing anxiety by schools that began to envision overseeing their own progressive programs, for less cost. In response to this anxiety and even after President Cheek lowered the membership fee from $4,000 to $2,500 annually, the hemorrhage of member schools continued.

Union was in some ways a victim of its own success, Cheek later noted, and rent needed to be paid for thirteen offices around the country. In addition, Cheek faced other problems almost from the start of his tenure. There was the nagging problem of what to do about revenue shortfalls based on tuition. Students who may have enrolled and then did not—or could not—follow through with payment of their tuition bills. What was worse, the shortfalls came even after many students actually paid their tuition and awaited twenty-five percent tuition rebates then offered by Union. But honoring the rebates depended upon prompt payments, which proved an increasingly elusive goal for students and one that was ultimately detrimental to the Union's fiscal well-being.

For the cash-starved Union, it was increasingly difficult to make do with less revenue. New programs—the lifeblood of educational experimentation—were increasingly expensive. Administrative expenses could hardly be trimmed in an environment that demanded closer attention, not less, to details. Meanwhile, a fretful faculty saw their reimbursable expenses not always restored on time, and worse, some promised monetary benefits not being paid at all.

For some of the problems, Cheek's hands were essentially tied by his sense of responsibility to students. "The institutional culture gave people a chance," he told journalism professor Michael Kirkhorn. Kirkhorn would later prepare a detailed account of the Union's descent into bankruptcy in 1978 and the aftermath of its reorganization.[94] Students who did not pay, for whatever reason, were still considered viable, worthwhile students, and deserving of the opportunity for which they had tried so diligently to avail themselves. But those students who did not pay, of course, were still simply being subsidized by those who did pay.

Cheek, as president of two Historically Black Colleges and Universities (HBCUs) before arriving at the Union, was well aware of the social and economic difficulties facing poor minorities. HBCUs struggled with seemingly intractable problems not affecting most mainstream white institutions: tiny size and limited funding, often received from various denominations of churches with limited resources; populations of students from less affluent backgrounds, often the first generation in their families to attend college; and more recently, the "brain drain" of both bright students and faculty to traditionally white institutions, an ironic consequence of the headway being made in the modern civil rights movement of the 1960s and 70s.

Cheek did manage to rout some of the myriad of problems characterizing his first full year in office (1977). He viewed that time as "a difficult and rewarding one" in his preface to the January 1978 report to the UECU community. The year had been "difficult in transition and rewarding in the discovery of a new identity that uses the strengths of over a decade of building," he wrote, and continued on a note of encouragement. "We have made a fresh commitment to our mission and have set out to use our experience and close working relationships to create better means of addressing the issues it represents."[95]

But he cautioned his audience against any complacency. "In spite of successes, there remain many unmet challenges and needs," which he intended to address "in the months and years ahead." His attempt three months later, in April 1978, to increase revenue by raising tuition—from $700 to $900 a quarter—set off a firestorm of angry complaints from students, one of whom bitterly complained about being charged tuition as high as that of an Ivy League school.[96]

Cheek's efforts to revamp the Union graduate program, announced that same spring, appeared promising; his March 1978 memorandum to the Union Graduate School Reorganization Committee—a select group of faculty—outlined six major points for the committee to follow.[97] But the effort suddenly lost momentum shortly after it began. Obviously frustrated by the obstacles which prevented necessary reforms, and perhaps weary after four years of grappling with systemic problems, Cheek soldiered on until a fateful visit by an NCA accreditation team in May 1978, when it became clear that the once-proud Union was on the verge of losing its candidacy-status for accreditation.[98] During that team's visit, Cheek resigned.

> I left because it was an ethical dilemma for me (if I stayed). Did I want intellectual integrity, or not?" Cheek recalled in 2014. "I left because the Union 'family'—a very close-knit family, and I was a part of it—wanted me to do things that I did not want to do. I was brought in to kick the family in charge, and reshape the destiny of the Union. But I finally decided I did not want to do that.[99]

Cheek's sudden departure shocked many at the Union. Decades later, rumors persist that the board terminated Cheek, but there are no board minutes to substantiate the rumors. Cheek remembers his departure as a voluntary one, although he has never elaborated on the precise issues which impelled him to resign. According to a later account by Graduate Dean Ben Davis, "the president [King Cheek] resigned in the middle of the NCA accreditation visit." According to Davis, "the chairman of the visit…called me out of the room and said, 'We have to go. We can't be on a campus where there's no president during an accreditation visit.' Which makes sense, so I took him to the airport."[100]

More than three decades later, however, Cheek looked back on his Union years with a touch of sadness: "The original mission of the Union that motivated me and others was never fulfilled. And it's important to understand why that never happened," he said in 2014. "If the original vision had remained intact and we had stuck to it, the power of the Union would be exponentially greater than it is today."[101]

"I decided not to do what the people of 'the family' wanted me to do," Cheek said. "It was that simple. When you sit your butt down in the president's seat, your challenges can be very real and very difficult. And yes, they can change."[102]

Jim Dixon, the UECU board chairman during Cheek's tenure, had only praise in his memoir for Cheek. "King Cheek ... (was) interested and experienced in educational change," and Baskin had brought Cheek in to help him solve the "serious problems" facing the Union, including supervising the graduate school, already "in financial distress" in 1974, Dixon wrote in 1991.[103] By the time Cheek became president, the problems had grown larger, and he was no longer "kicking up his heels about the prospects of presiding over UECU. He'd been there long enough to know that there were serious problems," Dixon wrote.[104]

A number of Cheek's top aides also resigned abruptly, leaving the school in a full-blown panic. One financial assistant left so quickly that a significant number of unendorsed, un-cashed checks were later found under the assistant's desk blotter by Ben Davis. Meanwhile, according to Graduate Dean Davis, the graduate school was losing "$50,000 a month via these policies that don't work" [and] "the money was the most poorly handled piece of the institution and plagued it."[105]

The old Union was simply coming apart at the seams, judging by both Dixon's and Davis's accounts, as member after member prepared to leave by the nearest exit.

## Kenneth W. Rothe

King Cheek's departure from the Union presidency in 1978 was in some ways a body blow, signaling that the consortium might be on the ropes after fourteen years of high hopes and notable achievements. But the trustees were still not ready to throw in the towel. In mid-summer, the beleaguered UECU board—now led by Ronald Williams of Northeastern Illinois, who had only recently succeeded Dixon as the dean of the graduate school—chose to make one last stand. The Union turned to an outsider, Kenneth W. Rothe, provost of Ohio's Bowling Green State University since 1973, as its new savior. Rothe himself likened the situation at the time to "being asked to save a 'burning ship'—a loosely organized institution neither successfully unorthodox nor able to find respectability in accreditation."[106]

Dr. Rothe, a physicist by training and an experienced academic administrator, came to the Union as its first acting president and provost, titles he would continue to hold until his departure four years later. He had no idea how long the task would take, he said in 2014. But he acted quickly, and forcefully. Within six months, he had managed to put the fire out, tow the damaged ship into dry dock, and help to design a plan to rebuild it. Whether that refurbished ship would ever again prove seaworthy was not yet certain, or how many passengers could be enticed back to sail on it, but what is certain is that Rothe's captaincy saved the day for others yet to follow.

"I can safely say that there was not one single aspect of the Union that was working," Rothe said in 2014. "It was limping. The fundamental academic problem at Union was a control problem. It wasn't whether the work being produced was quality work, but rather that you didn't *know* if it was quality work. The program design was good—but the delivery system was unclear. And the financial situation was just incredible."[107]

How Rothe came to Union was almost as intriguing as the situation he was called in to help resolve. "I was on vacation for a year, after a very difficult period at Bowling Green," Rothe recalled. "Art Spiegel called me somewhere in Pennsylvania and said, 'I think you'd like this place.' So I went and visited some of the Union sites. I'm a pushover for things like the Union—I don't like things that aren't changing and if you don't want to change, then don't hire me!"[108]

S. Arthur Spiegel, then a lawyer in private practice in Cincinnati, was aware both of the Union's bankruptcy struggles and Rothe's reputation for handling challenging situations. (Two years later, Spiegel would be confirmed as a federal judge, after being nominated by President Jimmy Carter.)[109] On Spiegel's advice, Rothe took the job, seemingly against all odds, and started commuting by car or private plane—he was also an accomplished pilot, and flew himself—to Cincinnati, as Union's part-time acting president and provost. For a time, he continued to teach at Bowling Green State.

By 1979, Rothe was working full time at Union and, as a lifelong problem-solver, had more than enough to keep him occupied. "I'm always taking on something that does not work, always a new mess, that might end up working but it's usually a people mess," he said in 2014. What he found at Union—besides the obvious difficulties that had led to his recruitment—was an institution worth saving, as well as some remarkable students, faculty, and staff.

"The *good* news about the Union was the people. The Union itself was a fascinating place, and it was created to be that way," he mused some thirty-five years after the fact. "There is an edge between creativity and craziness, and the Union was perched right on that edge. By contrast, most PhD programs are *quite* sane and *not* at all creative. Now to me, *that* is crazy."[110]

Michael Kirkhorn's careful account in *Change* magazine—the well-regarded publication started by the Union—of the difficult days of 1978 and 1979 offered a sobering reflection on the twin perils and promise of experimentation in higher education. "Experimental schools perform about as reliably as experimental airplanes, experimental economic policies, or soufflé recipes," wrote the respected journalist and college professor, himself a graduate of Union's PhD program, in opening his article.[111]

After a dark night of "extraordinary shakiness," including the dispiriting specter of federal bankruptcy court and public humiliation, it appeared that Union might at last have turned a corner. "[B]ut the question that remains is how an organization dedicated to educational reform can survive this decade of retrenchment while continuing to experiment."[112]

How the school had gotten itself into the nightmarish situation was still not exactly clear, even to Kirkhorn:

> Nobody understands exactly how the Union skidded into its crisis. Some say it unwisely continued to invest money and energy in the expansion of the University without Walls, disregarding competition from traditional colleges and universities that had seized upon the UWW example to introduce similar program at less cost to students. Others think the Union spent too much money on central

administration. Or grew too rapidly. Or that its leaders allowed their idealism to carry the Union with all its leakiness and good intentions into a decade where accountability would be the watchword. Others insist that there would have been no crisis if the embarrassing bankruptcy action had not been filed.[113]

Still, Kirkhorn's investigation found one explanation "more plausible" than most: human error. There seemed to be, according to Kirkhorn, flaws in a leadership that was good at some things—even most things—but not all. Perhaps, he wrote in early 1979, "the leaders of the Union, successful as innovators, simply never discovered a form of management that would have guided the growth of the experimental programs they invented."[114]

Kirkhorn's summary of the situation, while lacking clear evidence or on-the-record statements that could shed light on the precise roles played by any of Union's leaders, has nonetheless prevailed over the years as the most complete explanation of the confusing situation faced by the Union.

There is no doubt, of course, that the bankruptcy action brought matters abruptly to a head. Forced on Union by two faculty members of the Union Graduate School and five doctoral students, the decision to declare bankruptcy came after unpaid bills amounting to $300,000 had begun piling up in the central offices. The situation had forced Union leaders to face a stark choice: close the school's doors or regroup and operate under sharply revised practices.

Rothe and the UECU board did manage to persuade the federal bankruptcy judge, Burton Perlman, to let the Union "manage its own rehabilitation," offering it a certain amount of breathing room and face-saving time in which to learn quickly, rather than endure a court-appointed trustee as sought by the plaintiffs. But only days later, the North Central Association withdrew the Union's candidacy on evidence its team had compiled of Union's poorly-managed administration, weak financial operations, and unacceptable academic standards. In effect, this withdrawal aborted Union's quest for accreditation.

From his vantage point in early 1979, Kirkhorn concluded that Rothe's leadership had proved more pragmatic and constructive than that of his predecessors. "Though the situation looked grim at best" before Rothe's arrival, he noted that "the Union has begun a remarkable turnaround" under Rothe during its bankruptcy struggle by building up a cash surplus, hiring a controller and accounting firms, tightening budgets, shedding money-losing programs, and warning nonpaying students to pay up or be dropped.[115]

Rothe remembers arriving at Union to find a team from the US Department of Health, Education, and Welfare (HEW) already on the scene, investigating unsubstantiated rumors of embezzlement of federal grant monies. That federal team remained in Ohio for the next six months, but never found any evidence of wrongdoing, or indeed, of any missing monies. By the time that the HEW team left Cincinnati, its conclusion was that poor bookkeeping—and poor bookkeeping alone—had been the Union culprit all along.[116]

The grueling process of rebuilding could now begin in earnest. Weakened but still resilient, the Union would resume its difficult path back to accreditation. The reorganization plan presented by the Reorganization Committee in December 1978 and approved by the board's executive committee was announced by Rothe in January 1979; it provided an excellent blueprint, but only if it could be implemented successfully. That plan, slated to take effect within six months, provided "the framework within which the Union will operate for the following two years and beyond." The plan essentially organized the Union into four units: the Union West, based in San Francisco, CA; Union Midwest, in Cincinnati, OH; Union East, in Washington, DC; and Union South, in New Orleans, LA. Each regional unit would have its own faculty and maintain its own committees of faculty and learners; deans would head all but the New Orleans office, which, for the immediate future, would have a director.[117]

The number of UWW programs, already sharply reduced by phase out or transfer to other schools, would be reduced to two affiliates: Hispanic International University in Houston, TX, and the University of California, San Diego. (Those UWW programs at Flaming Rainbow, Stillwell, OK, and Universidad Boricua, New York, NY, were either in the process of or becoming separately accredited.) Undergraduate enrollment in other Union programs—to be administered by the four regional offices—was expected to be "significantly smaller than graduate enrollment," both because of the UWW downsizing and competition from similar programs at other traditional schools.[118]

The staff in Cincinnati was to be reorganized and all duties redefined; new school titles included a chief executive officer, executive vice president, controller, and two assistant deans. Although the Union would continue to use a "significant number of qualified part-time faculty," because of their recognized "critical and creative role within the Union," the largely part-time core faculty was to be replaced, as expeditiously as possible, with a faculty of full-time core positions "until the majority of all learners are directly served by a full-time core faculty member."[119]

It would take three years before Rothe and the board felt satisfied that they had accomplished the two critical goals established in 1978: emerging from bankruptcy, reorganized and with strict new mechanisms and guidelines in place; and once again, established on the path to regaining accreditation status from the North Central Association.

By 1982, Union was now ready to recruit a new leader, as Rothe prepared to bid farewell—to the school, if not to his new home of Cincinnati, where he and his family were now firmly established, and where they continued to live more than three decades later.

# Kenneth W. Rothe, PhD

ACTING PRESIDENT AND PROVOST, THE UNION FOR EXPERIMENTING COLLEGES AND UNIVERSITIES
*(UECU), 1978–1982*

Dr. Kenneth W. Rothe was appointed acting president of the Union for Experimenting Colleges and Universities in August 1978, succeeding Dr. King V. Cheek as UECU's leader. Dr. Rothe served as head of the Union until July 1, 1982, when Dr. Robert T. Conley took office as president.

Prior to his appointment as acting president of UECU, Dr. Rothe had served as provost of Bowling Green State University (BGSU) in Bowling Green, OH, since 1973. His earlier posts included adjunct associate professor of physics and associate dean of the college at the University of Pennsylvania (Penn) in Philadelphia between 1966 and 1973.

Rothe's father worked internationally with Mobil Oil, and the family moved locales frequently, including a long stint in England. After returning to the United States to complete his education, Rothe completed his PhD in physics in 1966 from the University of Rochester, NY. He received a Woodrow Wilson Fellowship and intended to teach as a college professor, but he eventually worked in college administration, both at Penn and later at BGSU.

While at Penn, Dr. Rothe was a prime figure in the reform of undergraduate programs, helping develop the College of Thematic Studies, the Freshman Seminar, and the Environmental Studies program.

During his tenure at UECU, Rothe led the school through the difficult period after its bankruptcy filing in 1978, and slowly began to rebuild the school's depleted staff. In 1979, the school moved its Union Midwest offices to the Provident Bank Building in Cincinnati, OH, where they remained until the early 1990s.

After leaving UECU in 1982, Rothe and his wife Julia remained in Cincinnati. They now have two children and three grandchildren, and have lived in the city for more than twenty years.

Since leaving UECU, Rothe has served as chief operating officer of FSCreations, Inc.; as chief financial officer and chief science officer for Allostatix LLC; and as vice president of business effectiveness for Standard Textile Co., Inc. He also served as associate professor of hospital and health administration at Xavier University during the 1990s.

He recalls being recruited for the UECU job by telephone by S. Arthur Spiegel, a well-known Cincinnati attorney and later US federal judge (appointed by President Carter in 1980), one of the UECU bankruptcy attorneys. Spiegel called him while Rothe was on sabbatical/vacation in Pennsylvania in 1978, after a particularly tiring year as BGSU provost. "I think you'd like this place (Union)," Spiegel told him. .

It proved to be a challenge. "I'm a pushover for things like the Union—I don't like places that aren't changing," he said in 2014. "And I can safely say that there was not one single aspect of the Union that was working (well) when I got there. It was limping."

"The fundamental academic problem at the Union was a control problem. It wasn't whether the work being produced was quality work, but rather that you did not know if it was quality work. The program design was good, the delivery system was unclear, and the financial situation was incredibly bad. The really good news about the Union was the people."

*"The Don Quixote
of the educational world"*

## CHAPTER 4: THE CONLEY ERA

Dr. Robert T. Conley—known universally as Bob—arrived at Union almost by accident, certainly not by his own design. Having already spent much of his academic career in Ohio, as dean of engineering at Wright State University in Dayton, he had no immediate interest in returning to Ohio from New Jersey.

He had been appointed president of Seton Hall University in South Orange, NJ, in 1977, the Catholic school's first full-time lay leader and the first lay alumnus to hold the job. At Seton Hall, President Conley reorganized and modernized the university's administrative and financial structure, breathing fresh air into the institution which had given him his own start twenty-five years earlier.

By 1982, that job had ended.[120] But Conley and his family had remained in New Jersey, completing renovations to the old family home while Conley contemplated his next steps. In 1982, an unnamed visitor from UECU appeared in the Conley's' living room with an unexpected, dramatic proposition: Would he be interested in taking over the Union presidency?

The Union was certainly familiar to Bob Conley. In the 1970s, Conley had persuaded his own assistant dean at Wright State, Lois Cook, to pursue a PhD at the Union, and he had served as her core advisor during her studies there, Doris Conley recalled. But the Union that he had known then no longer existed, in fact. It had gone through Chapter XI bankruptcy and reorganized itself, painfully but completely.

Once a member-supported consortium, supported by membership dues and external grants, Union was now a fully tuition-funded institution, struggling to reestablish itself as an independent school, but with a diminished enrollment, it was living almost hand-to-mouth. Its old dual-board structure of governance had been streamlined in mid-1980, into a single board of trustees—but one which now stood in dire need of an energetic new leader to lead the school back to glory.

In 1982, Bob Conley was asked to consider taking on that huge new challenge, but with very little promise of success, little job security, and little hope even of being paid regularly. Doris Conley remembers the visitor from Cincinnati in their living room in the late spring of 1982, coaxing her husband to consider the job. She also remembers the end result: Bob simply could not resist the challenge.

"We won't move for a year," Bob told her before he left to assume the precarious role. "If it doesn't work, well, then nothing's lost."[121] Doris would spend the next year in New Jersey in the family home, the home they had spent years renovating, now waiting patiently to see whether this new job would pan out.

Their daughter, Robyn, then a student athlete at Wright State, remembers traveling down to Cincinnati during the first year of her father's presidency—in 1982 and 1983—and remembers her father's occasional pessimism. "I don't know if this place can make it," he told her. "I will give it a year and if I can't help, I will move on." The struggles continued, but each time she returned, he seemed more positive, she recalled in 2001. "Then one day I remember him telling me, I think this place is going to make it."[122]

Doris Conley remembers that her husband kept an amazingly low profile during that first year in Cincinnati, and lived frugally. There wasn't always enough money in the Union accounts to pay his full salary, much less expenses, so to save money, he was living in a small motel frequented by blue-collar workers, the Treadway Inn on Central Parkway. "He didn't tell anyone there what he did for a living," she said in 2014. "They thought he was just another Average Joe. Then one day the Cincinnati newspaper put his picture on the front page, and the men he had been living beside for months just stopped talking to him because they found out he was a university president, and not really one of them."[123]

It wasn't easy, but Bob Conley stubbornly managed to win back those skeptical friends using skills gained in his own hardscrabble childhood in New Jersey. He had never lost his touch for the common folk, which sometimes made him appear to be a misfit in the stuffy, formal world of academia. But it was part of his being: unpolished but genuine. He was one of a kind.

Growing up, Conley had never been expected even to get into a college, much less to become a college president; his high school guidance counselor had predicted failure for the young man if he were to attempt such a path. But an unexpected sports scholarship in track and his own gritty determination proved that counselor wrong.[124] Three degrees in chemistry later—a bachelor's degree from Seton Hall and both a master's degree and PhD from Princeton University—he was well on his way to the upper ranks of academia: he became professor at Canisius College in New York; then he returned to Seton Hall; and from there went on to Wright State, first as dean of engineering and then as vice president, before reaching Seton Hall as president.

His decade at Wright State (1967–1977) had been a turbulent and demanding one, during which he served as founding dean of the school's college of science and engineering, later as director of planning for health affairs, and finally as vice president and director of planning and development. His successful efforts to establish Wright State's medical school and school of nursing are the stuff of legend. He was even briefly touted as the school's next president—a job he might have enjoyed, according to Doris Conley, but the truth was that his dreams lay elsewhere.

The top job at Seton Hall, his alma mater, held more appeal and offered more of a challenge, one he could not resist (a trait firmly built into his character). Before he left Ohio for Seton Hall in 1977, his friends at Wright State presented him with a small bronze statuette of a seated horseman, a famous chivalrous character (of hopeless cases) by Cervantes (from the late sixteenth-early seventeenth century, the Golden

Age of Spanish literature), engraved simply, "To Bob Conley…the Don Quixote of the educational world."[125]

It was a good-humored send-off, given only partly in jest, far more as a respectful sign of appreciation for a job well done. That horseman still sits in his living room, more than fifteen years after his death, the perfect tribute to a man who could not resist just one more challenge. He was, after all, the quintessential, real-life knight-errant in search of adventure—always seeking more impossible tasks to achieve, more dragons to slay, more honor to uphold.

After his "trial" year was up at Union, Bob Conley finally decided the time was right to move his family to Cincinnati. He was even able to leave the Treadway Inn for good after Doris found a modern house for them out in an eastern suburb of the city. The house came complete with a swimming pool, which the Conley family used regularly.[126]

Over the next decade, the Conley home gradually became a gathering point for all things Union—from staff parties to long meetings and strategy sessions—as well as a haven for the workaholic president, who kept his favorite office there.

## CONLEY AT UNION

Conley set to work with characteristic energy and drive, raising the funds to erase the Union for Experimenting Colleges and Universities' daunting debt and revitalizing the school's quest for accreditation. By 1983, he had restored a sense of calm and balance to the once fragile institution, after convincing the North Central Association to recommend continuation of the school's Candidate for Accreditation status. In 1984, the UECU celebrated its twentieth anniversary by holding its first national commencement ceremony in May, followed by a number of crucial reorganization steps recommended by Conley. In July, the University Without Walls (UWW) was renamed the Undergraduate Studies program. In September, the UECU undergraduate program in Florida was licensed by the State of Florida. In November, the UECU was licensed in the State of California at both the baccalaureate and doctoral levels.

But the crowning achievement, perhaps, of President Conley's first two years came in October 1984, when the NCA Evaluation Team recommended full accreditation for UECU—a goal few had believed humanly possible just five years earlier. The team recommended a "focused visit in 1986–87 on 'quality control in the undergraduate program and documentation of learning attainments throughout the Union,'" to be followed by the next comprehensive visit in 1989–90. The actual granting of accreditation by NCA in February 1985 was important, if somewhat anticlimactic, but it was one of a continuous parade of accomplishments by the reborn school.[127]

In mid-1985, President Conley announced the formation of the school's Institute for Public Policy. The baccalaureate program became the Undergraduate Studies Program. Next, the 1986 New Ventures Group began the creation of the Office of New Program Planning and Development, formalized in 1988.

By 1989, President Conley took great pride in announcing that "all prior institutional indebtedness had been reduced to zero," a decade after the

Chapter XI bankruptcy filing. Perhaps to mark the school's phoenix-like status, the board of trustees agreed in July 1989 to a new name for the school—The Union Institute—and its two major divisions: the Graduate School of The Union Institute and the College of Undergraduate Studies.[128] Later that same year, the renamed The Union Institute gained its reaccreditation, after a second successful NCA team visit in that fall.

In a special report to the Union community, issued to mark the school's twenty-fifth anniversary in 1989, President Conley announced that enrollment had climbed to more than 1,100 students in the fall of 1988, counting both active and interim learners at undergraduate and graduate levels. It was a breathtaking twenty-seven percent increase in just one year, yet another sign of the school's renewed vigor. The growth, which had "caused a good deal of recent concern" in some quarters, had already prompted Conley and his staff to begin planning for a stunning long-range goal: "an institution of approximately 1,500 graduate learners and double that number of undergraduate learners." [129] In short, four times as many students in the foreseeable future could be expected; that meant, among other things, that more room would be needed for both administrative and faculty offices and classrooms.

Until then, the school had continued to reside on two rented floors—21,000 square feet, described by the NCA team as "pleasant and spacious"—of a downtown Cincinnati high-rise office building, the Provident Bank Building at Seventh and Vine Streets, where it had moved its offices in 1979. But that accreditation team also expressed that the school lacked public recognition or community profile because of its obscure location, where it was unable to hold its own conferences and seminars. The report acknowledged, however, that Union was bound by the terms of its current lease until 1993.[130]

The team noted, with apparent approval, that the Union's board had recently decided to purchase the school's first permanent home: a building at 440 East McMillan Street in Cincinnati, to be renovated to house Union's administrative departments and the offices for both undergraduate and graduate schools. The building, built in 1921 by the Procter and Collier Company, a printing and advertising agency for the Procter & Gamble Company, had passed ownership in the 1930s to the founders of the Beau Brummell Ties Company (Beau Brummell, Inc.), where it was used as the design studios.[131] An investment of some $3.5 million for purchase, engineering studies, and remodeling of the building would be required.

The re-design by Cincinnati architects A. O. Elzner and George Anderson to "harmonize with the widely admired [Gruen] watch factory"— built on a site just across McMillan Street during World War I, known as "Time Hill." The Tudor Revival–style stone Beau Brummell building contained 50,000 square feet on four floors, along with a total of ninety-two parking spaces and "small but lovely grounds."[132] Its distinctive tower held water for a sprinkler system.[133] Under Dr. Conley, the building would become listed on the National Register for Historic Places.

For Bob Conley, who donned a hard hat and supervised the interior renovations himself, it was the dream of a lifetime—and it was now his new home. Conley spent much of the next two years systematically supervising the gutting and remodeling of the Beau Brummell building, overseeing each detail as Union prepared to inhabit its first permanent home. "He was thrilled with this building," his daughter said years later. "He drove my mom crazy with all the ideas for it. He loved visiting the renovation site ... he dealt with the architects, contractors, and workmen on every level of the project." In some ways, it was the marriage of two very personal visions—his lifelong hobbies of woodworking and renovations combined with his "visions and dreams for The Union Institute." Union had now become a full-fledged "member of the family," she recalled.[134]

The school's phased move into the McMillan Street headquarters began in 1990, with renovation and construction completed in 1995; landscaping and parking work continued until 1996.

But renovating buildings was just one part of the continuing transformation led by Conley: In 1990, the Union became the first university in the United States to establish an Office for Social Responsibility, located in Washington, DC. That office initially housed the Union's Center for Public Policy, adding its Center for Women by the end of its first year.

"We wanted to reexamine the role of service in American higher education," Conley explained in 1998. "In traditional institutions, the participation of faculty and members of the academia in work [that] serves the academic community has been interpreted as service. ... For the most part, that service is restricted. At The Union Institute, we began a discussion to look at that service component on a nationwide basis—to figure out ways of bringing together the various voices to change the conversation about service."[135]

Founding the Center for Public Policy was a Union alumnus who quickly became synonymous with the school's values and its national image: Mark Rosenman, who was hired under Conley as vice president for social responsibility. A former president of Beacon College (Leesburg, FL) in the early 1980s, Rosenman had studied at the Union graduate school under Goodwin Watson and Jim Dixon in the early 1970s and continued to teach as a graduate faculty member after arriving at the Union.[136]

The Center for Public Policy was one of several innovative programs begun under Conley's leadership. Others included the school's joint program in community-based education with the United Teachers of Dade County, FL, then one of the nation's largest teacher unions, launched in September 1992. A separate program, started in July 1995, was geared toward encouraging professors and administrators at the nation's Historically Black Colleges and Universities—collectively known as the HBCU Initiative—to complete the Union's doctoral programs.[137]

Perhaps Conley's proudest accomplishment came in 1992 and 1993, when The Union Institute was twice named to the list of "America's Best Colleges" for the annual survey of the top 204 universities in the country in the *U.S. News & World Report*. The popular survey cited statistics in such categories as "selectivity" of the student body, overall financial resources, and the degree to which each school "supports a high-quality, full-time faculty." In addition, "the level of student satisfaction" was ranked highly according to each listed school's graduation rate.[138] Even if the "reputational score" assigned to schools on the *U.S. News* list was based on academic reputation rather than academic quality, the survey still demonstrated that The Union Institute was back in a big way. A mere decade after its bankruptcy, the Union was flourishing and drawing accolades from many observers.

Conley took the achievements in stride, expressing appreciation in a prepared statement for the "high marks by our peers and colleagues" but characteristically looked forward rather than at the past: "Our efforts in the years ahead will lie in fine-tuning existing programs while initiating and revamping new ventures. As we continue to grow, our reputation—I hope—will precede us."[139]

In 1996, with the completion of work at 440 East McMillan Street, Conley announced next phase of expansion of The Union Institute campus: the purchase of the building directly across McMillan Street, formerly known as the Gruen Watch building, where renovations began in 1998. Built in 1917, this Tudor-style building, like Union's Brummell building, was also listed on the National Register of Historic Places. Occupied by several subsequent owners since the watch factory's sale in the 1950s, the building needed extensive work to be restored to its original state.

After documenting the design features of the hunting lodge upon which the factory had been originally modeled, Conley's team began the task of faithfully restoring "Time Hill" to its original design. At the same time, The Union Institute also "invested heavily in improving the mechanical systems, creating a twenty-first century space in an early twentieth-century building," according to a 2009 article.[140] The distinctive building contained more than 35,000 square feet, enough to assure sufficient room for expansion of both the school's growing graduate programs, duly renamed the Graduate College in 1997 with two programs: the School of Interdisciplinary Studies in the Arts and Sciences and the School for Professional Psychology. [141]

By the end of 1998, The Union Institute had also begun exploring ways to expand its presence internationally, into both the Caribbean region and across the Atlantic, in Africa. The joint program envisioned by Conley with the English-language University of Buea in Cameroon, certainly the most ambitious project yet on The Union Institute's drawing boards, would have been another historic move. But it was still in the planning stages in March 1999, when Bob Conley's era came to an unexpected, jarring close.

On a particularly snowy day in March 1999, Bob Conley ordered the Union to close its doors for the day, after deciding the roads were too dangerous for his staff to use. He stayed away himself, working in his home office. Among other projects, he was busily planning his forthcoming trip to Cameroon. Forbidden by Doris to shovel the driveway, he watched through his window as others cleared it.

In mid-afternoon, he interrupted his schedule to go outside and retrieve the day's mail. Not long after retrieving the mail, Conley slumped over in his home office chair, the victim of a massive heart attack. He did not survive.[142]

Bob Conley, who had considered retirement in passing, had made no real plans for it. And although the Union did boast a strong second layer of leaders, including vice presidents Susan Wood, Mark Rosenman, and Peter Hollister, Conley's untimely death and his close-to-the-vest operating style left a sudden vacuum of power at the very top of the school's leadership structure. It also left many unanswered questions about his plans for the future.

Conley would be eulogized by many at his memorial service four days later, among them a successor at Seton Hall University—its current chancellor, the Very Reverend Thomas R. Peterson, O.P.—and Tom Ost, longtime secretary to Union's board.[143] Ost, a personal friend to Conley, recalled his beloved mentor in a moving, eloquent personal tribute in his funeral eulogy. It was reprinted weeks later in the Union's *Network* magazine:

> Our savior was not the usual fictional model of a hero. He was a chemist. Actually he was an Alchemist.
>
> Who but an Alchemist (one of those medieval figures who turned dross into gold) could have made the Union of 1982 into today's Union Institute, a force in American higher education? It was then bankrupt, unrecognized. In the words of the prophet Isaiah, "despised and rejected."
>
> Besides alchemy, Bob practiced another science, one of his own invention. I like to call it Zen Accounting. To the chagrin of the accountants and auditors, he endowed numbers with mystical characteristics and wove them in ways that defied the conventional wisdom. And to the further frustration of the accountants, it worked.[144]

His last great adventure had lasted seventeen years. The Don Quixote statue, once a whimsical tribute from friends, now became the fitting epitaph for an intensely private man forced by fate to play a very public, very nontraditional role.

A year before his death, Bob Conley had been asked by an interviewer to look into the future of his beloved school. His response, condensed here, was in many ways prophetic:

> I think you will see a change in the way that you deliver the educational services to our learners, and that will be largely due to emerging new technology which will facilitate our ability to work with additional people. ... We've moved beyond the University Without Walls concept and have looked at a whole myriad of mechanisms by which instruction should be delivered and can be delivered, and we're sorting through all those. ... I think that the next decade will be a fascinating period of change as we adopt more and more technological process to serve our learners.[145]

# Robert T. Conley, PhD *(1932–1999)*

PRESIDENT, THE UNION FOR EXPERIMENTING COLLEGES AND UNIVERSITIES *(UECU), 1982–1989*

PRESIDENT, THE UNION INSTITUTE *(TUI), 1989–1999*

Dr. Robert T. Conley, fourth president of the Union for Experimenting Colleges and Universities, succeeded acting president Kenneth W. Rothe as UECU leader in 1982. He headed the Union and its successor, The Union Institute, until his death in 1999.

Conley, a 1953 graduate of Seton Hall University in New Jersey, was that Roman Catholic's school's first lay president from 1977 to 1979. A chemist by training, he held a master's degree (1955) and PhD (1957) in chemistry from Princeton University, and he served as a chemistry professor at Canisius College (Buffalo, NY) and Wright State University (Dayton, OH), where he then became dean of the school of engineering.

Involved in the early years of the space race through the Gemini program, Conley had worked to develop a chemical heat shield to protect space capsules from burning on reentry to the Earth's atmosphere. He was also responsible for analyzing rival technology of Russia's Soviet Union.

When Conley arrived at Union in 1982, the school faced severe financial difficulties and a shrinking enrollment. By 1989, when the school changed its name to The Union Institute, Conley was widely recognized as the driving force behind the school's remarkable turnaround: then free of debt; boasting a student enrollment of more than 2,000; and expanding its programs across the nation. Union was also the proud occupant of its first real "campus" in Cincinnati's Walnut Hills neighborhood, with Conley's visionary acquisition and restoration of the Beau Brummell Tie and Gruen Watch manufacturing buildings on East McMillan Street.

"Bob changed the culture of the university profoundly," remarked Mark Rosenman, Union's professor emeritus and then vice president of social responsibility (1991–2001) in 1997. Conley modestly described himself that same year as "just a good fit here." Conley said "the university was academically sound" when he arrived, "just undernourished." (Weathers 1999)

Conley's legendary energy and ubiquitous enthusiasm were unmistakable, displayed in frequent visits to Union's undergraduate centers in Miami, Los Angeles, Sacramento, and San Diego; his development of the undergraduate Center for Distance Learning; and his spirited reorganization of the school's Graduate College.

In seventeen years as Union's president, he initiated partnerships that led to programs designed to meet the needs of such academically under-served groups as law enforcement professionals, substance abuse counselors, elementary and high school teachers, and faculty at Historically Black Colleges and Universities (HBCUs). At the time of his death, he was busy directing Union's reaccreditation process; continuing to supervise restoration of the Gruen building; and preparing to visit the African nation of Cameroon, where Union's new joint doctoral program with the University of Buea—a newly-established, English-speaking university—was awaiting its launch.

Fay H. Williams, chair of The Union Board of Trustees, described Conley in 1999 as "always mindful of the university's mission of combining scholarship with social awareness and action." He "worked ceaselessly to strengthen and expand the university's academic offerings," she said, and constantly sought "new ways to bring educational opportunities to those not served by mainstream academic institutions."

Conley's survivors included his wife, Doris, son Bryan Conley, his daughters, Debra Henderson and Robin Barbiea, and five grandchildren.

*The family requested that memorial contributions be made to the*

**ROBERT T. CONLEY SCHOLARSHIP FUND**

**AT THE UNION INSTITUTE**

## CHAPTER 5: TRANSITIONAL LEADERS
## MERVYN L. CADWALLADER AND JUDITH A. STURNICK

What was all too apparent after Bob Conley's unexpected death was that no one at The Union Institute had been prepared for life after him. He had made no real plans for his retirement, and members of the board were stunned by the enormity of the task of filling their leader's shoes. There was no successor in the wings, no simple transition drawn up—and unthinkable as it was—there was no choice but to move on.

Veteran graduate faculty member Mervyn Cadwallader, executive vice president of The Union Institute from 1988 to 1995, and a former college president and administrator elsewhere, was quickly selected as acting president, effective April 1, 1999. He was assisted by continuing vice presidents Wood, Rosenman, and Hollister. Cadwallader would hold that post for a year, stepping down in April 2000.[146]

In a long interview weeks later with the *Network* magazine, Acting President Cadwallader described his previous service under Conley as that of "a pinch hitter. If there was something that needed to be done, a problem that needed to be solved, or if some unexpected opportunity appeared out of nowhere, he would use me. ...What I was doing was a combination of trying out new programmatic ideas and putting out fires."[147]

By early 2000, Cadwallader had hoped to "hand over a healthy, happier Union Institute to the next president. That means restoring formal faculty governance, shepherding us through a successful reaccreditation … getting us reauthorized by the Ohio Board of Regents [and] fostering team work to build trust," he said during his interview. He had already created two task forces—one to focus on enrollment, recruitment, and marketing, and the second to focus "on our vision of the future." Both would need to draw "on the ideas, brains, and energy of everyone in the Union community" as well as "interact and inform each other's work."[148]

"I'd like to present the new president with a list of good things accomplished and a list of good things that are underway," he said. But he expected a few bumps along the way. "We're the second largest graduate school in the state of Ohio… and that makes some others very, very nervous. … If you're going to grow The Union Institute, then you have to develop a strong reputation out there. … I think we start by building a really great institution, and then getting the word out."[149]

By the time The Union Institute's next leader took over, the long period of introspection occasioned by Conley's death had produced a dramatically different environment for the school—and an unexpectedly dramatic choice for its top role.

As 1999 drew to an end, the Union prepared to enter the new twenty-first century—but without a permanent successor to Bob Conley yet named. During the transitional leadership of acting president Mervyn

Cadwallader, the board had begun considering a significant number of possibilities—more than forty candidates in all, according to board chair Fay H. Williams—but with no hint as to when a final decision would be announced. In the spring of 2000, after Cadwallader stepped down from the acting post, the board finally named its surprise choice.

The next president would be the Union's first female leader, and by far the most controversial in the school's four decades: Judith A. Sturnick, a veteran educator and scholar with ties to midwestern and northeastern schools, then serving as vice president of the Office of Women in Higher Education at the American Council on Education in Washington, DC. Sturnick's credentials were impressive: president of Keene State College in New Hampshire and the University of Maine at Farmington; an experienced professor, president and principal of her own private leadership firm; coauthor of *Women at the Helm* (1991); and an international consultant. She held a PhD in English from Ohio State University, a master's degree from the Miami University (Ohio), and a bachelor's degree from the University of North Dakota.

Williams and others saw the Minnesota native as "an excellent match for the university at this time in its history," a leader whose "experience and knowledge, coupled with her passion for our mission, will guide the university to new heights in years to come." As with both her predecessors, Bob Conley and King Cheek, Dr. Sturnick promised a fresh, innovative approach to a school eager to revitalize its experimental past and continue Union's traditions of national leadership in education. Williams and the board expressed certainty that "the entire Union Institute community will be as excited as the Board is at this result."[150]

Her selection seemed a farsighted and inspired choice, one promising to provide a strong role model for the Union's female students and faculty after nearly four decades of a more patriarchal model. Sturnick herself expressed "great respect for the core values that have guided the university since its founding … and for its mission which has clearly made a difference in higher education." She also looked forward, especially, to working with "both the undergraduate and graduate faculty, since it is my long-held belief that the faculty is the heart of any academic institution."[151]

After taking office in June 2000, Dr. Sturnick immediately began implementing her plan for the future, while establishing a unique leadership style that charmed most, though not all, of her new colleagues. In October 2000, she described the school in her first commencement address as "the fertile field of invention in which is seeded and grown a bounty of daring ideas about global change, connection, culture, and leadership" and issued a daring mandate that would soon bear tangible fruit: "continuously… renew that field of experimental and innovative educational practice."[152]

As she recalled in 2014, "I had plans to distill a vision. I went there with lots of dreams, lots of visions."[153] Her very personal vision, which she described in some detail to a Vermont journalist a year later, required a new kind of educational institution to usher in "a global leadership development program," one that would take people "where they are and lead them into a doctoral program." The three prevailing models, in her view, included the traditional four-year residential college—still very important, if no longer preeminent—and an emerging model of the "virtual university," with most of its offerings available online via distance learning, a process using the Internet to link students and instructors. But according to Sturnick, such virtual universities embodied severe limitations, as she told journalist Nat Frothingham: "lockstep courses, a specified curriculum," and a reluctance to accept the value of the adult learner's life experience. Only a third model—one that she believed The Union Institute already represented, and which needed only refinement—could answer the very real needs for leaders in the twenty-first century.[154]

In early 2001, she would give shape to that challenge with arguably the most radical leap forward of the Union's entire history: the acquisition of a complete college campus in Montpelier, Vermont. The proposed purchase of Vermont College—a proud, storied, and progressive college in the heart of the tiny Vermont capital—immediately bolstered Union's enrollment figures, adding 1,000 students from around the world as well as the first master's-level programs in the school's history. Yet it also added significantly to Union's capital and operating costs; the price paid by Union, never publicly specified but rumored to exceed $10 million at the time, was easily the single most expensive undertaking in its history, dwarfing the purchases of the two buildings on East McMillan Street in Cincinnati.

Norwich University had originally sought as much as $21 million for the Montpelier campus and surrounding acreage. Founded in 1834 as Newbury Seminary, Vermont College had gradually become a junior college (1941) and a four-year institution in 1958. In 1972, after years of discussions with Norwich, Vermont College had then merged with the private military school in neighboring Northfield. The merger had enabled the larger school "to expand its academic base, extend its offering to women, and add a non-military lifestyle," according to the Norwich website.[155] To invigorate the arrangement further, Norwich had begun admitting women to its programs in 1974, and in 1981, purchased four adult-centered alternative education programs from yet another area school, Goddard College in Plainfield. Goddard, among the founders of the original UREHE, had since fallen on hard times.[156]

Yet while the two schools' missions were complementary, the fit had never been quite perfect, and by January 2001, Norwich leaders had grown disenchanted, announcing plans to divest the university of the Montpelier campus: still profitable, but apparently no longer central to its future.

Dedicated exclusively to low-residency programs, Vermont College emphasized interdisciplinary, multicultural studies in the humanities and social sciences. The school offered baccalaureate studies in nine fields—humanities, social sciences, environmental studies, holistic health, spirituality, creative writing, fine arts, women's studies, and teacher licensure—plus a Master of Arts program (with fifteen majors) and separate specialized master's programs in education, fine arts (visual), and fine arts (writing).[157] Its campus boasted eleven buildings, including the central College Hall, completed in 1872; three dormitories; a dining hall; classroom buildings; and the small but well-regarded Gary Library.

Acquiring Vermont College was certainly a daring step for The Union Institute, which already owned two buildings in Cincinnati and administered centers in rented facilities in Florida and California. Its purchase would necessitate an extensive capital campaign, place a heavy new burden on the small school's administration, and add a significant increase to operating costs. Convincing the board of trustees to embark on this venture was not easy, as Sturnick told Frothingham: there was resistance to having a physical campus for the quintessential "University Without Walls," a name long since dropped but heavy with nostalgic significance. The crucial, deciding factor appeared to be the ready-made master's programs—which The Union Institute had never before offered—and the college's thriving undergraduate program, called the Adult Degree Program, from its founding at Goddard College. Both programs promised a continuing source of revenue.[158]

The agreement in principle was announced with no small fanfare in mid-April 2001, before being approved unanimously by the Union board of trustees on June 15, 2001.[159] In a letter dated April 17, 2001, President Sturnick described the "wonderful news" to "Friends of the Union Institute" in lofty, metaphoric words:

> It is a classic case of two institutions with parallel missions and values uniting to strengthen each other. Just as two lenses that make up a pair of glasses act in synergy to create improved sight, the pairing of two cutting-edge institutions brings our vision for the future into sharp focus, and provides countless opportunities for program development and faculty enrichment ... and another beautiful, historic setting in which to hold seminars, colloquia, and other events.[160]

The acquisition of Vermont College brought with it several added attractions, including a separate smaller facility in Brattleboro, VT—

which The Union Institute would now operate as its Brattleboro Academic Center—and at least nine core and adjunct faculty members who held doctorates from Union Institute. Its traditions would continue to be honored, along with its existing name, extended now to "Vermont College of the Union Institute & University."

But perhaps most importantly, The Union Institute family would gain an invaluable new administrator: Richard Hansen, PhD, senior vice president of Norwich and a Vermont College administrator since 1989, was named provost and executive vice president. In this role, Hansen had responsibility for the day-to-day operations of Vermont College. Hansen's ties to Union were underscored by his previous service as vice president for public affairs (1981–1989) at Thomas A. Edison College in Trenton, NJ, where his boss had been Dr. George Pruitt, a Union alumnus (PhD 1974), who had recently succeeded Fay H. Williams as chair of the Union board of trustees.

Hansen joined at least two other new administrators at Union in early 2001: Associate Vice President Emily Harbold, PhD, formerly assistant vice president at Texas Women's University, who oversaw academic affairs at Union; and Roger H. Sublett, PhD, interim vice president for national undergraduate programs at Union and formerly director of the Kellogg Foundation's National Leadership Program.

With Vermont College officially transferred to Union ownership in October 2001, Sturnick and the board then agreed to a name change that would reflect the school's expanded operations and twenty-first century vision. What had begun in 1964 as the Union for Research and

Experimentation in Higher Education and renamed twice, as the Union of Experimenting Colleges and Universities (1974), and then The Union Institute (1989), had now became Union Institute & University. It signaled a new day in the school's ever-evolving tradition.

"I felt that we had a wonderful, visionary opportunity to combine Vermont College and the Union in a very progressive and innovative way," Sturnick recalled in 2014. "Like it or not, mergers and consortiums and those combinations are, ten years from now, going to save higher education. I had hoped, back then, that the Union would succeed and set the pace for the future."[161]

She recalled developing close relationships with students and faculty members alike. "I cultivated the faculty because I was very interested in what they were doing," she said afterward. "And I spent a long weekend with one class to see what their learning experience was like. My way of leading has always been to make myself as well-known as possible, to alumni boards, to student groups."[162] But even as the ink dried on the name change, the relationship between President Sturnick and the once-unanimous board began to unravel.

Her health suddenly undermined by a painful back ailment—which eventually required extensive surgery, bone grafts, and a lengthy recuperation—Sturnick began spending less time in Cincinnati, under doctor's orders to limit her flying.

Her rapport with the board began to deteriorate quickly, just as her health worsened. An increasingly distant relationship with the new board chairman, George Pruitt, who took over duties from Fay H. Williams in

April 2001, did little to help the situation. For his part, Pruitt recalls only that the situation between Sturnick and the board "wasn't a good fit, it wasn't good for either of them. The idea of acquiring Vermont College was sound but the economics did not work, and that exacerbated the situation."[163]

In the summer of 2002, just two years after her triumphant appointment, Sturnick resigned as president to return to her home in Massachusetts, to undergo surgery and then to endure almost two years of recuperation. Her career in higher education, however, was still far from over. After her recuperation, she went on to become the interim president of Montserrat College of Art in Beverly, MA, from 2007 to 2009. There, for two years she raised money and helped construct new buildings, one of which was named for her. "It was very reassuring, to tie a wonderful bow on my career," she said.

Today, Dr. Sturnick continues to write and lecture, and she runs her own consulting firm in Naples, Florida. The meaning of leadership continues to be her mantra, one borne out in her forthcoming book, tentatively titled *Fire In My Soul*. Her new book will deal with the meaning of community, government, and family, and will document the revelational experiences of many modern leaders.[164]

# Mervyn L. Cadwallader, PhD

ACTING PRESIDENT, THE UNION INSTITUTE
*(TUI), 1999–2000*

Dr. Mervyn L. Cadwallader served as acting president of The Union Institute from April 1, 1999, until the spring of 2000, after the death of

Robert T. Conley. Cadwallader's successor at the Union helm was Dr. Judith A. Sturnick, who took office in June 2000.

A sociologist by training, Dr. Cadwallader holds a PhD in history, sociology, and anthropology from the University of Oregon at Eugene. He also holds bachelor's and master's degrees in history from the University of Nebraska.

Prior to becoming acting president of Union, he had served as executive vice president of The Union Institute under President Conley. Previously, he had been academic dean and professor at San Jose State College, as well as professor of sociology and humanities and director of its Experimental Program in Humanities and Science, and as president of Western New Mexico University, a small public school in Silver City, NM. He taught sociology at the State University of New York—College at Old Westbury and at Pratt Institute in Brooklyn, NY.

In 1971, he was selected as one of three founding deans of the new Evergreen State College at Olympia, WA, a public liberal arts college, where he helped design one of the nation's most enduring nontraditional programs of higher education. It was at Evergreen that Dean Cadwallader emerged as Evergreen's "first acknowledged visionary," according to an MIT study of the school in the 1990s. Cadwallader's "strength was his ability to envision and articulate the academic objectives for Evergreen," in the words of colleague Richard Jones.

While serving as vice chancellor of the University of Wisconsin—Platteville in 1983, Cadwallader wrote that "the modern research university has wiped out general and liberal learning in American colleges and universities" ("The Destruction of the College and the Collapse of General Education," *Teachers College Record*, Summer 1983). He called for the need to restore a sense of purpose to colleges which offer general education, along with the importance of placing a proper value on teaching.

He once recalled an unusual childhood and well-traveled early life: "I was born in a leper colony in central east Africa, and once I was going to be a medical missionary. I almost fell off a mountain near the Cape of Good Hope just before I sailed to Boston on a very slow freighter. My family stopped in Glendale, California, and settled in Lincoln, Nebraska. The U.S. Navy sent me to the Great Lakes, San Diego and Oakland. I took a train back to Lincoln, drove to Oakland, and then moved to New York City, and would you believe it—Eugene, Oregon!"

He also described himself as "an intellectual in spite of myself and always a habitual teacher. I became a sociologist by accident and a dean by mistake. I love to teach… I am impatient with events that are slow and administrators that are slow."

*After serving as Union's acting president, Cadwallader continued to teach, most recently at the University of Phoenix and its School of Advanced Studies. He resided for years in the Flagstaff, Arizona, area, where he worked as an independent education management professional.*

# Judith A. Sturnick, PhD

| President, | President, The Union |
| The Union Institute | Institute & University |
| (TUI), 2000–2001 | (UI&U), 2001–2002 |

Dr. Judith A. Sturnick assumed the presidency of The Union Institute in June 2000. During her tenure, the school was renamed Union Institute & University. She held the Union post until her resignation in August 2002, after which Dr. Roger H. Sublett was named acting president.

At the time of her appointment, Dr. Sturnick was vice president of the Office of Women in Higher Education at the American Council on Education, Washington, DC, and widely recognized for her expertise in the dynamics of organizational change. From 1987 to 1993, she had served as president of Keene State College in Keene, NH, where she led fundraising for a substantial campus construction program and served as president of the University of Maine at Farmington (1983–1987).

Her other posts included vice president for academic affairs at Southwest State University, Marshall, MN, and interim provost for Paul Smith's College, Paul Smiths, NY. During her career, Dr. Sturnick has consulted with the United Nations on global leadership issues and co-founded a major leadership development program in Sweden.

A native of Blue Earth, MN, she holds a PhD in English from Ohio State University; a master's degree in English from Miami University (Ohio); and a bachelor's degree in English and history from the University of North Dakota. She is the co-author of two books: *Women at the Helm: Pathfinding Presidents at State Colleges and Universities* and *Women's Studies: A Guide*.

During her years at Union, the school expanded its programs with the purchase and incorporation of the Vermont College campus in Montpelier, VT, and the creation Union's new Master of Fine Arts program. During her tenure the school adopted its current name, Union Institute & University, to describe more fully its status as a degree-granting, post-secondary educational institution.

After leaving the Union presidency, Dr. Sturnick later served as acting president of Montserrat College of Art in Beverley, MA, from 2007 to 2009. She currently lives in Naples, FL, where she was one of four co-founders of the Entrepreneur Society of Naples.

An accomplished pianist, Dr. Sturnick studied piano for twelve years and received art lessons from her uncle, who was a professional artist. Her preferred medium is pastels and she loves to draw.

"I love what music, art—the arts in general—bring to the quality of life for us individually and for the culture as a whole. It changes the way we look at the world and at ourselves," she said in 2007.

*"Engage, Enlighten, Empower…"*

## CHAPTER 6:
## ENTERING THE MODERN ERA: ROGER H. SUBLETT

In less than eighteen months at his new school, Roger H. Sublett had quickly proved his merits, first as interim vice president for national undergraduate programs beginning in May 2001, then as provost and chief operating officer, a position he assumed by the end of the same year. The skillful administrator had years of experience, both in academia and private foundation work, as well as a PhD in American history from Tulane University (New Orleans). When he was tapped as the acting president of Union Institute & University in August 2002, he added yet another substantial title to a growing resume as the board undertook a nationwide search for a permanent leader.

His calming influence and steady hand quickly impressed the board in the wake of President Sturnick's departure, and reassured both students and alumni alike. Few observers were surprised when in April 2003, Dr. Sublett emerged as the board's consensus choice for the permanent job.

George Pruitt, chairman of the board, was a strong supporter. "When Roger came in, his plate was pretty full; it was a roller-coaster," Pruitt recalled in 2014. "Union's achievements had been extraordinary, but there were issues and some unrest."[165] Pruitt left the board in late 2003, but remembers his time and accomplishments with obvious fondness—and a sincere appreciation for the talents of Roger Sublett, in whom he recognized the strength of leadership the now-struggling school needed. He was convinced, in fact, that Union Institute & University might not have survived without Sublett's capable leadership at a critical point in its history, saying that "Roger should be remembered as the reason why Union Institute & University is still here today."[166]

Indeed, the issues facing the new president were complex and chronic, including a less than ideal relationship between the faculty and the administration, insufficient revenues to support the school's recent expansion, and the distant thunder of a looming dispute with the Ohio Board of Regents over issues related to compliance and accreditation. Such issues were a tall order for anyone, but Dr. Sublett's decade at the Kellogg Foundation had given him a unique perspective on leadership across the spectrum of American education, business, and public service.

Dr. Sublett had held several positions at the University of Evansville in Indiana—as associate vice president, dean of the college of graduate and continuing studies, and director of special programs—before joining the Kellogg Foundation in 1989. He had also served as a classroom professor, in addition to stints as executive vice president of the Association for Continuing Higher Education (1984–1989) and president of the Coalition for Adult Education Organizations (1989–1990).

Pruitt, the president of Thomas Edison State College in Trenton, New Jersey, was familiar with both Union's traditions—as an alumnus (PhD 1974)—and its board president, having been recruited to the board by former chairman Leo Goodman-Malamuth in the mid-1980s. When he took over from Fay H. Williams as chair in April 2001, Pruitt became only the third board chairman in sixteen years. Williams had served in that capacity since 1992, after seven years of leadership by Goodman-Malamuth.

As the board's vice chairman at the time of Bob Conley's death, Pruitt had worked closely with Williams during the transition. Pruitt had warm praise for the late president Conley, who "should be remembered as the savior and builder of the Union, and in his entirety, one of the reasons the institution is here today," he said. The problems facing his successor four years later, however, stemmed from an almost-inevitable, if ironic, decline at the end of Conley's tenure. "The institution was not growing and changing, and the board wasn't as engaged as it should have been," Pruitt declared. "Some things should have happened but did not happen. Bob Conley did not want to recruit a new provost if he was going to retire; he had held both jobs." As a result, no successor was on hand at the time of Conley's death, and the school's management culture was ineffective without a strong leader.[167]

Pruitt stepped into his new role with confidence and determination. "I had a strong background in institutional governance and was a voice for good government practices. I saw part of my role as the designated government person on the board to get the board to understand the roles of the president and the chairman," he said in 2014. The board needed to learn "to leave to the president—and the faculty—the things that were within their purview."[168]

As Pruitt and his successors began to shape this new understanding of shared responsibility, the new president's background gradually revealed a gritty determination to solve problems in an orderly and sequential fashion. Pruitt's successor as board chairman, attorney Cheryl Foley, recalled the early days of Sublett's tenure with a wry practicality. "It was a difficult period," at least at first, with the board often "preoccupied with trying to help Union survive," she said in 2014.[169]

"Sometimes it wasn't clear that we would survive," she explained. "Back in those days, we were always turning over rocks and finding new problems. Roger used to say he was afraid to find one more rock because he knew that underneath it was another problem."[170] But his steadiness and unflagging optimism helped guide the school through.

The son of a coal miner, Sublett had spent much of his childhood on a farm in rural Arkansas. Neither of his parents had finished their own education, his mother having left school as a teenager to take a job as a newspaper typesetter before marrying his father at age seventeen. His own academic talents had helped him find an unexpected opportunity in higher education, which quickly became a revelation. "Back then there weren't many opportunities in that part of Arkansas. But I was fortunate enough to be able to go to the University of Arkansas, and it opened up my life," he recalled a decade later.[171]

> I grew up on a farm, where we had to be self-sufficient to survive. I had to understand theory and develop practical skills, to make decisions that affected the family's livelihood, and these were skills that served me well in school and throughout life. So I learned early to take risks and not be afraid of those risks. I actually learned a lot more from failures than from my successes. The key for me is to remain open to the challenges that life brings you.[172]

After becoming the first member of his family to graduate from college, Sublett had expected to become a high school teacher. But his talents in graduate school had soon steered him in a different direction, to the University of Evansville, where he found what would become his greatest life-changing challenge and cause: adult education.

"I graduated from the University of Arkansas with a history degree, and I thought I would be happy teaching high school history. But after I moved over into administration, I became involved in programs designed for adults," Sublett recalled in 2015. "I learned about the flexibility of adult education. It had been existing on the periphery, as continuing education, in the educational world." Sublett now saw the full range of possibilities and was soon "touching every aspect of life in the university, all of the academic programming across the entire university."[173]

His experiences at Evansville paved the way for his jump to the W. W. Kellogg Foundation of Battle Creek, MI, in the late 1980s, to serve as director of the foundation's Kellogg National Fellowship/Leadership Program. Founded in 1930, the Kellogg Foundation was among the ten largest American foundations of its kind when Sublett left in 2001, with foundation and trust assets amounting to $7.3 billion (in 2005). Among the primary beneficiaries of its grants are child-centered programs, seeking to "support and build upon the mindsets, methods, and modes of change that hold promise to advance children's best interests generally."[174]

With broad experience in academia, university administration, and foundation work, Sublett seemed admirably suited to the presidency of a university seeking to serve working adults. "When I had the chance to come to Union, I brought a lot of different experiences to the job. I had come to Union from the Kellogg Foundation, and I was aware of the school's national reputation and the creative genius of its founders," he said. Yet the Union environment he encountered on arrival had apparently not kept pace with the changes in the political and educational climate since the 1980s.[175]

"The school seemed to have gotten off track, somehow. I was particularly surprised to find issues of quality in the leadership. The people here had serious challenges at the undergraduate level. So my job at first was about trying to correct many of those problems," he added.[176] As interim vice president for National Undergraduate Programs, Sublett was asked early on by the board to travel to California, survey the poorly-functioning academic center in Los Angeles, and close it down if necessary.

"My first trip was to Los Angeles, where our center had only thirty-seven full-time undergraduates enrolled. It was not succeeding," he said in 2014. "But I recommended not closing it, and I think it was the right decision. Today, more than a decade later, we have about 300 students enrolled, and its criminal justice program is thriving."[177]

Among Dr. Sublett's first actions in his new position at Union was to hire new deans for the school's academic centers in California: specifically, Dr. James Rocheleau in Sacramento, later dean of both California centers, and Dr. Marie Bogat at the Miami Beach center in Florida. "I worked very hard to stabilize the undergraduate program," he recalled in 2014. "I kept delivering that message, seeking to inspire people who shared my vision and optimism about what we could do with it—whether it was through the tutorial method, classroom learning, or distance learning."

Both programs were quickly stabilized and began to grow, just as Sublett began to assume more responsibilities in Cincinnati. His positive, surefooted approach in dealing with a succession of problems in a measured fashion has won him high praise from those who have chaired the board of trustees since his arrival. Pruitt, who served as chair until December 2003, and his successors—attorney Cheryl Foley (2004–2007), business leader Lisa Lorimer (2008–2010), and educator Betty Overton-Adkins (2010–2012)—all expressed great confidence in Dr. Sublett's leadership over the decade.

Lisa Lorimer, a Vermont College alumna recruited to the board by Sublett, had equally positive memories of her work with the president and the school. A successful businesswoman in her own right, she became chair in January 2008. She vividly recalled Union's "fundamental business model change" during a period she calls "the storm, the changeover."[178]

"We changed from people—'customers' who came in and stayed five to seven years, or longer at the doctoral level—to students who were coming in with credits and completing undergraduate programs, staying perhaps one and a half years at most," she said in 2014. "So that meant we had to have more customers, more learners. We were all surprised at this change."[179]

Dr. Overton-Adkins, a university professor and administrator in Michigan, succeeded Lorimer as board chair in 2010. A former colleague of Dr. Sublett at the Kellogg Foundation, and a longtime personal friend, she praised him for being "dogged in his vision. This has been hard work, and some people would have said hang it up and look elsewhere. I am just so glad he stayed."[180]

Sublett's tenure has certainly not been without its challenges, as he often reminds his listeners. "The years from 2003 to 2005 were pretty volatile ones," he recalled in 2014. "The US Department of Education had serious questions about our financial aid programs and Title IV programs. The Higher Learning Commission got involved." The school's struggle to maintain its accreditation amid a lengthy dispute over compliance with the Ohio Board of Regents, cited by Pruitt, consumed much of the next three years. But despite the crisis, the school never lost its accreditation, as Sublett is quick to point out, and eventually received full renewal of accreditation from the Higher Learning Commission in 2010.

The ensuing financial crisis, which led to the departure of many longtime faculty members, was another obstacle. "One of the major challenges we faced was our need to reduce the faculty by a significant number, partly due to financial pressures, caused by the need to maintain a balanced budget," Sublett said. It was not easy for either the faculty or Sublett. "So many of the faculty had been there for a lot of years, and here I was asking them to make great changes, something that many of them could not do, either psychologically or academically."[181]

The reorganization and revamping of the school's doctoral-level programs was yet another challenge, resulting in the creation of the current cohort program after the phasing out of the previous structure, which became known as the "pre-cohort" program before it ended in 2012. But Union maintained its dedication to its long-time students, helping a significant number of pre-cohort students—more than 550, by Sublett's tally, including some who had spent a decade or more at Union—finish their doctoral degrees before that program ended.

"When I came in 2001, the PhD program was under great stress, from the Ohio Board of Regents, the Higher Learning Commission, and the US Department of Education. But we were able to negotiate our paths through those pressures and come out with a revitalized PhD program at Union," Sublett recalls.[182]

Preserving and refining the doctoral program was one of the school's three top achievements after his arrival, in his opinion. Being reapproved in 2009 for accreditation for a full seven years, given the school's past challenges, was another. The third was the school's ability to "attract high-quality young faculty members—not just in undergraduate education, but also in our graduate program. They have great vigor and ability. There is a new enthusiasm and an entrepreneurial spirit in our setting."[183]

The graduate program continues to be revised to meet current needs. Among the changes announced in 2015 were to the EdD program—an experimental program which is now being merged into the existing PhD program, as a fourth major—and the decision to "teach out" the more recent PsyD program, which will end in 2018, when its last students graduate. The introduction of a new master's-level program online—the Master of Science in Organizational Leadership (MSOL)—is a sign of Union's continuing desire to innovate.

"It is not just another MBA program, but instead develops a new kind of leader who understands the current world of innovation, sustainability, solution-building, and entrepreneurship," Sublett said. The MSOL program embodies the philosophy of a new generation of leaders, such as Craig Hickman, author of *Mind of a Manager, Soul of a Leader*, one book high on Sublett's recommended reading list. "During the 1980s and the 1990s, everybody talked about excellence—but really, what is emerging today is something more: the pursuit of integration and balance."[184]

"I am convinced we are giving life to Dr. Baskin's vision from the early days," Sublett said. "Union Institute & University is still changing higher education for the better."[185] Ever the historian at heart, Sublett remains on the watch for new frontiers to explore. Recalling Professor Frederick Jackson Turner's essay on the American frontier in the West, Sublett is looking these days over the higher educational mountain: "We're going to change the face of higher education [in order] to further the education of adult students around the world. Right now, I have a team looking at it for Union" by exploring "how to expand Union Institute & University into global education."[186]

The changing face of Union Institute & University itself, however, was mirrored in President Sublett's single most controversial decision: how to deal with the nagging problems of real estate and the overhead costs of maintaining the significant number of buildings which housed Union Institute & University in Cincinnati and Montpelier. The decision to dispose of all the school's real estate ended an era of acquisition—begun by Bob Conley in 1989 and continued by Judith Sturnick in 2000—and was viewed with skepticism in some quarters.

"In 2006, Union's Board of Trustees made the bold decision to divest real estate property in order to redirect Union's creative and financial resources to our two top priorities—our people and our academic programs," Sublett wrote in 2009. "The decision to focus on people and programs instead of bricks and mortar is deeply rooted in Union's tradition. Known historically as a 'university without walls,' Union is proving once again that we believe education has no boundaries, particularly not physical ones."[187]

Still, the process of selling the school's property was often grueling. After much discussion, the board of trustees decided in April 2006 to put all of the school's real estate holdings on the market, including the Vermont College campus. A quick, initial expression of interest from the University of Vermont in Burlington, which was considering opening a Montpelier branch of the state's largest public university, raised hopes on all sides. Those hopes dissipated almost overnight amid a practical debate over the high cost of the transition and operation.[188]

"I think the board recognized fully that this was actually a significant opportunity and an exciting one," UVM Provost John Bramley told journalists in May 2006. "But that it was just an additional area of work both in the planning and operation that we couldn't take on at this time."[189] In November 2006, another group of potential buyers—the newly-formed Friends of Vermont College, composed of nearly one hundred of their alumni—publicly pegged the sales price at $17 million.[190] Group spokesman Genie Rayner declined to say how much her group had offered, but expressed the group's hope that, if successful, they could continue to maintain it as an academic institution.

In early 2007, a deal was announced with yet another group, the new Vermont College of Fine Arts (VCFA), headed by its acting president, Thomas Christopher Greene, who had recently been administering the MFA program in writing for Vermont College and the Union Institute. The sales price, not disclosed until 2008, was $10.75 million.[191] President Sublett, who signed the letter of intent, expressed delight with the arrangement, which called for Union Institute to lease back space from the VCFA for the next five years.

Foley, the Union board chair at the time, called the sale a "win-win situation" for all. "We are so pleased to work together with our counterparts at the Vermont College of Fine Arts, and set the stage for a new educational center that will serve not only central Vermont but also students across the nation who will participate in the many offerings available on the historic campus," Foley told journalists in 2007.[192] The deal was expected to be completed by mid-2007, but did not go through for another year.

Under the agreement, Union planned to "lease office, classroom, dormitory, and meeting space from VCFA and operate its educational offerings as one of UI&U's six national academic centers," including its undergraduate adult degree programs; the master's and new MA Online programs; and the Master of Education degree program. In addition, Union Institute & University agreed to continue operating the school library in a shared arrangement to serve both its students and VCFA students.

The sale was finally concluded in June 2008.[193] Union Institute & University continued to operate its programs at Vermont College until 2013, when it transferred all its programs to the Brattleboro Academic Center. Back home in Cincinnati, the buildings on McMillan Street—the greatest physical legacies of the Conley era—were sold during the nationwide recession, which began in 2008. The old Gruen Watch Building on McMillan Street was sold in 2009, for an estimated $2.7 million, to Lighthouse Youth Services, a multiservice agency providing social services to children, youth, and families, according to a Cincinnati business website report.[194]

The main administration building, which continues to house administration offices, an academic center, and the graduate programs, was sold to an investment group at about the same time for an undisclosed sum. Union Institute & University now leases the McMillan Street property from the new owner. "It wasn't our first choice," Union's chief financial officer Ed Walton, who has since retired, told journalists at the time. "A sale and leaseback is never as good as owning. But if you need the capital you invested in the building, it can work. You have to have some driving rationale to do it."[195]

In 2015, Union has now returned to its original tradition, in at least one major respect: it no longer owns property. The school once again rents all its office space, preferring to spend its revenue, as much as possible, on educating its students, rather than on maintaining buildings. Now debt-free, the school has emerged in far healthier financial shape than a decade ago. The doctoral program—whose stability and growth are due, Sublett says, in large part to the indefatigable efforts of its former dean, Dr. Larry Preston, who created and developed it—continues to attract a strong crop of applicants.

Overall, Sublett's long list of accomplishments—and the steady, surefooted handling of each difficult challenge—has become a reassuring tribute to the board's decision to appoint him in 2003. His successful recent efforts to begin building the school's first real endowment are a source of great pride to Sublett. Substantial grants for scholarship funds from the Western & Southern Financial Group and the Helen Steiner Rice Fund totaling $500,000 were pledged in early 2014.[196]

As always, Sublett's focus remains firmly on the future. "I believe it goes back to the kind of interdisciplinarity that Sam Baskin talked about: how do we find greater harmony among groups and professional relationships, how do we protect the environment? By building programs for the future, by engaging at a different level."

Above all, Union Institute & University must continue to strive to be "flexible, nimble, and effective in managing scarce resources during its next half-century. Our undergraduate programs need to be much more diverse. We need to expand our faculty."[197]

And as Union Institute & University prepares to enter its second half-century, that future appears bright. Its current academic offerings include bachelors of science degrees for twelve majors; a bachelor of arts for a major in psychology; a master of arts degree for six majors; a master of arts degree for a major in clinical mental health counseling psychology; and a doctoral program, now with four major areas of study. About 1,100 students are enrolled in more than a dozen undergraduate and graduate programs at its academic centers in Cincinnati, Brattleboro, North Miami Beach, Sacramento, and Los Angeles. The school's staff and faculty number more than 400 full-time and part-time members through its various centers and programs.[198]

Many of Union's students today are adults seeking undergraduate degrees, much as envisioned by Tim Pitkin in Goddard's adult degree program, and by other founders of the Union of Research and Experimentation in Higher Education a half century ago. But in a somewhat surprising reversal of the original model—which attracted mostly working doctoral students, but comparatively few undergraduates—the school now generates more than two-thirds of its revenue from undergraduates.

Many of today's Union students are working women. Many juggle the intertwined lives of being single parents and meeting other obligations including volunteer and church work. Eventually, these women could become the first in their families to graduate from college. Inspired by their example, Sublett obtained a seedling grant of $50,000 from the Kellogg Foundation to offer scholarships to such women. "If you really want to help lift children out of poverty, start by educating their moms," he told Kellogg in his grant proposal. It worked.[199] Sublett has since helped catalyze creation of a total scholarship fund totaling more than $1 million, including large grants from the Western & Southern Financial Group, the Charlotte Schmidlapp Fund of Fifth Third Bank, and the Helen Steiner Rice Fund of the Greater Cincinnati Foundation that funds the Virginia Ruehlmann Fellowship for women pursuing graduate degrees. Another $250,000 grant named for Eugene P. Ruehlmann, the beloved former mayor of Cincinnati, funds a fellowship in his name for doctoral students pursuing public policy.

What does President Sublett see for the future? More change, both in the field of higher education and in Union's response to its students' needs. "Really, I hope we will retain the transformative and experimental model at Union," he said in 2014. "I think higher education is in for big changes, not just in the next twenty-five years, but in the next five."[200]

The future for Union may involve a more specialized approach: certificate programs in a variety of fields, for students with degrees who may want certificates in a different field—perhaps in maternal child health or the lactation program, among others. Dr. Sublett is already seeking partners for these programs and hopes to double the school's enrollment in the next few years.

To be self-sustaining, Union Institute & University needs roughly 2,500 students enrolled in all its programs, he believes. The school's current full-time equivalency tally in the latest semester—for the winter of 2014–2015—was around 1,100, with most of these students being enrolled in the undergraduate programs operated at Union's centers in California,

Florida, and Vermont, as well as in Cincinnati. The PhD program alone needs about 300 students, in Sublett's view, or roughly three times the current level.

To attract the new students Sublett envisions, he plans a multifaceted effort. First, he will ask for help from Union alumni: each graduate will be encouraged to "recruit at least one new student." Another facet will be a totally redesigned website, considered among any school's most effective recruitment tools in the twenty-first century: "an advancement that has increased our technological ability to respond, the new website is much more user-friendly, with shorter descriptions, and does a much better job of communicating very quickly." According to Sublett, "people are not going to read through 800 pages, but they may well read 800 words."[201]

Marketing, of course, can be a complicated and expensive task. "It's an uphill battle. We must commit more marketing dollars, but we also have to be smarter about how we use our budget: will it be on radio and television, or somewhere else?" Sublett asserted. "We currently spend about $1.5 million a year on marketing, out of a total budget of $24 million—not quite 10 percent—but compare that to much larger schools, with budgets above $100 million."[202]

Other approaches to growth include distinctive niche programs. "For one, the Martin Luther King, Jr. Studies specialization in the PhD program—helping to extend the legacy of the revered civil rights leader—will continue to draw strong applicants to Union Institute & University. In addition, innovative partnerships with other schools, such as that with Columbus State Community College in Ohio, should be particularly useful for increasing enrollment. With this partnership, for instance, a student's third year of college study can be finished by enrolling at Union Institute & University directly on the Columbus campus. "We hire the faculty, and the students pay community college rates; then for their fourth year, they study at Union and pay our tuition rates," Sublett said of the resource-sharing arrangement.[203]

The cost of any student's education remains an ever-important factor. Much attention has been paid in recent years to student debt, which averages about $26,000 for public four-year graduates, and $29,000 for private school graduates—less than many observers might expect, but still a significant sum. "We have to engage in that national debate over whether a college education is valuable," Sublett declared. "Higher education is about careers, about jobs, yes, but it is also about transforming students' lives and then transforming their communities and organizations."[204]

In the end, Sublett believes, it will also come down to one memorable connection between faculty and student, a connection which then generates the word-of-mouth promotion that lingers most indelibly: "Our faculty has to be committed to caring for each student. We want our students to look back and say they stayed because of this particular faculty member."

Through more than a decade on the job, Sublett's deliberate style of leadership—based on six principles outlined in a 2009 address to UIU alumni, and excerpted below—has proved useful in facing each new challenge:

1. Courage: "None of us want to fail. And we often limit the effectiveness of our efforts as a result. [W]e should understand that it takes courage to acknowledge our fears and work through them."
2. Self-knowledge: "Leadership is not about power or position—it is relational and all about relationships."
3. Focus on others: "Leaders look for the strengths in their colleagues and spend time helping others enhance these strengths for the benefit of the entire organization."
4. Attitude: "In addition to being knowledgeable in their position, the best asset in any employee is a great attitude. ... When it comes to good employees, give me one with a great attitude."
5. Behavior: "Choose to behave in a way that makes others feel as if they are the most important people in the world. Always be truthful in your presentation. ...tell the truth and you don't have to remember anything else."
6. Communication: "Obviously, how you deliver a message is important. Besides being sincere and clear, it helps to have a positive message. Of those three, clarity is often the most difficult to achieve." [205]

The motto of today's Union Institute & University might well be summed up in the three words one often hears within and beyond its Cincinnati headquarters: Engage, Enlighten, Empower. The phrase is now the kernel of the university's mission statement. Born of a two-year, university-wide self-study that began in 2007, the words were adopted from the institutional vision and quickly became the theme of the self-study. That was no coincidence, Sublett wrote in 2009, for "these words have served to focus the university community on our institutional strengths and distinctions—and also describe the transformational learning process so often cited by learners, faculty, and alumni alike."[206]

Fifty years after its founding, Union Institute & University continues to "give life to Dr. Baskin's vision," in Sublett's view, as an example of innovation and experimentation. So what precisely can today's Union Institute & University teach other schools?

"The competency-based model is catching on, and much of traditional higher education has come around to our model. In one way, what we might once have called non-traditional is now traditional," Sublett said in 2015. "As just one example, other schools that once built libraries with fixed hours are making their libraries accessible twenty-four hours a day. Here, everything in our library is online."

"In a sense, then, the world has come back to Union."[207]

# Roger H. Sublett, PhD

| ACTING PRESIDENT, THE UNION INSTITUTE & UNIVERSITY *(UI&U), 2002–2003* | PRESIDENT, THE UNION INSTITUTE & UNIVERSITY *(UI&U), 2003–* |
|---|---|

Dr. Roger H. Sublett became acting president of Union Institute & University in August 2002, succeeding Dr. Judith A. Sturnick. In April

2003, he was named president of Union Institute & University by the board of trustees.

Before becoming president, Dr. Sublett had served since 2001 as Union's interim vice president for national undergraduate programs, provost, and chief operating officer. Prior to coming to Cincinnati, he had served at the W. K. Kellogg in Battle Creek, MI, including a decade as director of the Foundation's National Fellowship/Leadership Program. Earlier, while at the University of Evansville (Indiana), he had served as associate vice president for academic affairs, as dean of the College of Graduate and Continuing Education, and as director of special programs in the College of Alternative Programs.

He holds a PhD with a focus on American history from Tulane University in New Orleans, LA. He also holds a bachelor's degree and master's degree from the University of Arkansas. The editor of *Leading from the Heart: The Passion to Make A Difference* (2001), Sublett is also the author or co-author of three other books and numerous articles.

A former chair of the Commission on Lifelong Learning at the American Council on Education in Washington, DC, Dr. Sublett has also been a senior fellow in the James McGregor Burns Academy of Leadership at the University of Maryland, College Park; a senior scholar at the Center for Ethical Leadership in Seattle, WA; executive vice president for the Association for Continuing Higher Education; and president of the Coalition for Adult Education Organizations.

His wife, Dr. Cynthia Sublett, teaches nursing at Xavier University in Cincinnati. They have three grown daughters and three grandsons.

As a leader with a passion for history, Dr. Sublett is committed to upholding Union's fifty-year tradition of innovation in its role as a change agent in higher education: to foster the shared values of "integrity, diversity, and flexibility."

# EPILOGUE: THE UNION LEGACY IN THE OUTSIDE WORLD

Any institution of higher education may be justifiably proud of its graduates, and prouder still of their accomplishments. For its graduates are the living proof of the school's academic effectiveness, and in turn a practical recruiting tool for future students.

Union Institute & University is no exception to the rule, having conferred degrees upon thousands of its students since its creation in 1964. Its first degrees were awarded in the 1970s, and the school now boasts some 15,500 alumni.

Among these Union graduates are a current member of the US House of Representatives; the prime minister of a Caribbean nation; a leading American social worker and philanthropist; an acclaimed public historian and chair of a well-known art museum; and a distinguished US businessman and philanthropist:

- Illinois congressman Daniel (Danny) K. Davis (PhD 1977), a former high school teacher and Cook County, IL, commissioner, has served the seventh district of Illinois in the US House of Representatives since 1997.

- Portia Simpson-Miller (BA 1997), a former social worker and longtime member of the Jamaican parliament, is currently serving her second term as Jamaica's prime minister, having been elected in both 2006 and 2012.
- Constance McCatherin Silver (PhD 1983), a well-regarded psychoanalyst, artist, and trustee of New York University (NYU), who, with her husband Marty, has donated $50 million to NYU in support of their alma mater's McSilver Institute for Poverty Policy and Research in the NYU Silver School of Social Work .
- Clarissa Pinkola Estés (PhD 1981), Jungian psychoanalyst, poet, *cantadora* (story teller), and best-selling author of *Women Who Run With the Wolves: Myths and Stories of the Wild Woman Archetype*. Founded the Guadalupe Foundation and was the first recipient (1996) of the Joseph Campbell "Keeper of Lore" award.
- Elizabeth A. Sackler (PhD 1997), a public historian and advocate for Native Americans, founded the Elizabeth A. Sackler Center for Feminist Art at the Brooklyn Museum in New York and was recently selected as that museum's first female chair.
- The late Sidney Harman (1918–2011; PhD 1973), philanthropist and businessman, was a co-founder of Harman Kardon—a leading manufacturer of home and car audio equipment—and chairman of Harman International Industries. Also served as US Undersecretary of Commerce in 1977 and 1978, during the administration of President Jimmy Carter.

Union graduates since the 1970s also have included a small but singularly significant group: future college presidents. Like so many of their fellow alumni, who have gone on to success in the worlds of academia, business, government service, and public office, these college presidents are reminders of the core values upon which the Union was founded, and of the call to excellence which they and so many others have answered. Hundreds of others have gone on to serve academia in equally distinguished positions, as professors, deans, and vice presidents.

But perhaps more than any other single group of alumni, those Union graduates who have gone on to head other US institutions of higher learning symbolize both the potential value of nontraditional adult education and the collective fulfillment of the promise that the ten founding schools of the original Union sought to pass forward to succeeding generations.

BEGINNING IN 1972, DOCTORAL DEGREES HAVE BEEN AWARDED BY THE UNION TO THE FOLLOWING FUTURE COLLEGE PRESIDENTS, HERE LISTED ALPHABETICALLY BY SURNAME:

#### —— DANNY R. GOEHRING — (PhD 1974)

Former president of Flaming Rainbow University, Tahlequah, OK

#### —— GRACE S. JONES — (PhD 1985)

Recently retired president of Three Rivers Community College, Norwich, CT; former president of the College of Eastern Utah, Price, UT.

#### —— ARTHUR KEISER — (PhD 1998)

Current chancellor of Keiser Collegiate System, For Lauderdale, FL.

#### —— VIRGINIA LESTER — (PhD 1972)

Former president of Mary Baldwin College, Staunton, VA

#### —— MARAVENE LOESCHKE — (PhD 1975)

Recently retired president of Towson State University, Towson, MD; former president of Mansfield University of Pennsylvania.

#### —— SCOTT D. MILLER — (PhD 1991)

Current president of Virginia Wesleyan College; former president of Bethany College, Bethany, WV and Wesley College, Dover, DE; former president of Lincoln Memorial University, Harrogate, TN.

#### — Clark Moustakas — (PhD 1986)

President emeritus and Co-Founder, Center for Humanistic Studies Michigan School of Professional Psychology, Farmington Hills, MI.

#### — Kerry Moustakas — (PhD 1993)

Former president of the Center for Humanistic Studies/Michigan School of Professional Psychology, Farmington Hills, MI.

#### — Laura Palmer Noone — (PhD 2000)

CEO of Piccolo University; former president of the University of Phoenix, Phoenix, AZ; former president of Potomac College, Washington, DC.

#### — Maureen O'Hara — (PhD 1976)

Former president of Saybrook Graduate School, San Francisco, CA.

#### — Michael E. O'Neal — (PhD 1983)

Former president of H. Lavity Stoutt Community College, British Virgin Islands (BVI).

#### — Stanley V. Paris — (PhD 1984)

Founding president/chancellor of the University of St. Augustine for Health Sciences, St. Augustine, FL.

#### — George A. Pruitt — (PhD 1974)

Current president of Thomas Edison State College, Trenton, NJ.

#### — Thomas P. Rosandich — (PhD 1978)

Founding/current president of the United States Sports Academy, Daphne, AL.

#### — Mark Rosenman — (PhD 1977)

Former president of Beacon College, Washington, DC

#### — Jane O'Meara Sanders — (PhD 2000)

Former president of Burlington College, Burlington, VT.

### Mark Schulman — (PhD 1985)

Former president of Saybrook University, Santa Barbara, CA; former president of Goddard College, Plainfield, VT; former president of Antioch University of Southern California.

### Charles W. Simmons — (PhD 1978)

Founding/current president of Sojourner-Douglass College, Baltimore, MD.

### Eleanor J. Smith — (PhD 1972)

Former chancellor of University of Wisconsin–Parkside, Somers, WI.

### Leon Tarver — (PhD 1995)

Former president of Southern University System, Baton Rouge, LA.

### Barbara Vacarr — (PhD 1993)

Former president of Goddard College, Plainfield, VT.

### Judy E. Walters — (PhD 2006)

Former president of Diablo Valley College, Pleasant Hill, CA; former president of Berkeley City College, Oakland, CA.

### Gary S. Wheeler — (PhD 2007)

Former president of Glen Oaks Community College, Centreville, MI; current member, Board of Trustees of the Higher Learning Commission, Chicago, IL; former president of Gogebic Community College, Ironwood, MI.

# UNION INSTITUTE & UNIVERSITY

*a look at centers around the country*

### NEW ENGLAND ACADEMIC CENTER
28 Vernon Street, Suite 210,
Brattleboro, VT 05301-3669

### LOS ANGELES ACADEMIC CENTER
6701 Center Drive West, Suite 120
Los Angeles, CA 90045-1535

**FLORIDA ACADEMIC CENTER**
16853 N.E. Ave, Suite 102, North Miami Beach, FL 33162-1746

**SACRAMENTO ACADEMIC CENTER**
160 Promenade Circle, Suite 115
Sacramento, CA 95834-3725

**NATIONAL HEADQUARTERS —
CINCINNATI ACADEMIC CENTER**
440 East McMillan Street, Cincinnati, OH 45206-1925

# APPENDIX A: CURRENT TRUSTEES

*Current Trustees, Union Institute & University*

Members of the Union Institute & University's Board of Trustees are selected for their commitment to the University's purpose and mission. Members are active and involved participants in the governance of the institution, and committed to its growth and development. The Union's Board of Trustees meets four times each year, in January, April, July, and October. Current members of Union Institute & University's Board of Trustees are included below, along with their affiliations and information therein:

### Donald Feldmann, JD (Chair)

President and CEO
Rippe & Kingston Capital Advisors, Inc.
Cincinnati, OH

### Richard N. Aft, PhD*

President
Philanthropic Leadership
Cincinnati, OH

### Roger Allbee

CEO, Grace Cottage Hospital
Secretary of Agriculture (retired)
Townshend, VT

\* Alumnus/Alumna of UI&U

**Lee Binder, PhD***

Director
Ben Gamla Charter School
Miami, FL

**Kim Byas, PhD***

Regional Executive
American Hospital Association
Chicago, IL

**Kay E. Goss, CEM**

President
World Disaster Management, LLC
Alexandria, VA

**Gladys Gossett Hankins, PhD***

President/Global Management Consultant
Telora Victor, Inc.
Cincinnati, OH

**Sandra L. Lobert**

President and CEO
Hospice of Cincinnati
Cincinnati, OH

**Shekhar Mitra, PhD**

President, InnoPreneur LLC
Consulting Partner, Yourencore
Senior Vice President, Global Innovation (retired)
Procter & Gamble Company
Cincinnati, OH

**Betty Overton-Adkins, PhD**

Vice President, Academic Affairs, Professor of English
University of Michigan
Ann Arbor, MI

* Alumnus/Alumna of UI&U

**Katherine Prince**

Senior Director, Organizational Development and Foresight
KnowledgeWorks
Columbus, OH

**Edgar Smith**

Chief Executive Officer
World Pac Paper, LLC
Cincinnati, OH

**Roger H. Sublett, PhD (Secretary)**

President, *ex officio*
Union Institute & University
Cincinnati, OH

**Dennis Tartakow, PhD***

Editor in Chief
Ortho Tribune
Marina del Rey, CA

**Christine Van Duelmen**

Executive Director/Conference Coordinator (retired)
International Council for Innovation in Higher Education
Toronto, ON

**Virginia Wiltse, PhD (Immediate Past Chair)***

Director and Vice President
Caring Response Madagascar Foundation
Cincinnati, OH

* Alumnus/Alumna of UI&U

# Appendix B: Board Chairs, 1965–2014

| Board Chair | Term | Affiliation |
|---|---|---|
| *Union for Research and Experimentation in Higher Education* | | *(1964–1972):* |
| **Royce S. Pitkin, PhD** (1901–1986) Plainfield, VT | 1965 – 1969 | President, Goddard College |
| **Rev. Reamer Kline, ThD** (1911–1983) Annandale-on-Hudson, NY | 1969 – 1970 | President, Bard College |
| *Union for Experimenting Colleges and Universities* | | *(1970–1989):* |
| **Rev. Reamer Kline, ThD** (1911–1983) Annandale-on-Hudson, NY | 1970 – 1974 | President, Bard College |
| **James H. Werntz, PhD** Minneapolis, MN | 1974 – 1976 | University of Minnesota |
| **James P. Dixon, MD** Yellow Springs, OH | 1976 – 1978 | President, Antioch College |
| **Ronald Williams, PhD** (1927–1985) Chicago, IL | 1978 – 1985 | President, Northeastern Illinois University |
| **Leo Goodman-Malamuth II, PhD** (1924–2013) University Park, IL | 1985 – 1989 | President, Governors State University |

*The Union Institute* *(1989–2001):*

| | | |
|---|---|---|
| **Leo Goodman-Malamuth II, PhD.** (1924–2013) University Park, IL | 1989 – 1992 | President, Governors State University |
| **Fay H. Williams, JD** Indianapolis, IN | 1992 –2001 | Attorney |
| **George A. Pruitt, PhD*** Trenton, NJ (Apr.–Nov.) | 2001 – 2001 | President, Thomas Edison State College |

*Union Institute & University* *(2001 – )*

| | | |
|---|---|---|
| **George A. Pruitt, PhD*** Trenton, NJ | 2001 –2003 | President, Thomas Edison State College |
| **Cheryl Foley, JD** Cincinnati, OH | 2004 –2007 | Attorney |
| **Lisa Lorimer, MBA** Montpelier, VT | 2008 –2010 | Consultant |
| **Betty Overton-Adkins, PhD** Spring Arbor, MI | 2010 –2012 | Spring Arbor University |
| **Virginia R. Wiltse, PhD*** Cincinnati, OH | 2012 –2014 | Director and Vice President, Caring Response Madagascar Foundation |
| **Donald Feldmann, MBA, JD** Cincinnati, OH | 2014 – | President, Rippe & Kingston |

\* Alumnus/Alumna of UI&U

# Appendix C:
## Members of the Board of Trustees, 1971–2015

*Union's records for the Board of Trustees prior to 1976 include Executive Committee minutes only. Therefore, the lists generated from these minutes may have inadvertently omitted some Trustees. Lists of Trustees prior to 1971 are not available.*

*Until 1980, The Union had two Boards: the Board of Trustees as described above and a Membership Board, composed of the representatives of consortium member institutions.*

## Members of the Board of Trustees —— 1971/1972

| | |
|---|---|
| **Trustees** | Samuel Baskin<br>King V. Cheek<br>James Dixon<br>John Elmendorf<br>Reamer Kline<br>P.J. Manion<br>Otis Shawo<br>James Werntz<br>Gerald Witherspoon<br>Robert Woodbury |

## MEMBERS OF THE BOARD OF TRUSTEES — 1972/1973

Trustees
| Samuel Baskin
King V. Cheek
James Dixon
Ralph Gauney
Tom Jones
Reamer Kline
Otis Shawo
James Werntz
Gerald Witherspoon

## MEMBERS OF THE BOARD OF TRUSTEES ——— 1973/1974

Trustees
| Samuel Baskin
King V. Cheek
Bert Dillon
James Dixon
Ralph Gauvey
Tom Jones
Reamer Kline
Alan Mikels
Jerome Sachs
Otis Shawo
James Werntz
Robert Woodbury

## MEMBERS OF THE BOARD OF TRUSTEES — 1974/1975

| | |
|---|---|
| Trustees | Samuel Baskin<br>James Dixon<br>Ralph Gauvey<br>Archie Hargraves<br>James Mullen<br>Eugene Ouellette<br>Jules Pagono<br>Carol Pollis<br>James Werntz |

## MEMBERS OF THE BOARD OF TRUSTEES — 1975/1976

| | |
|---|---|
| Trustees | Samuel Baskin<br>James Dixon<br>Ralph Gauvey<br>James Mullen<br>Jules Pagano<br>James Werntz<br>Robert Woodbury |

## MEMBERS OF THE BOARD OF TRUSTEES — 1976/1977

Trustees
Leon Botstein
  *(replaced 11/76 by Jerry Cohen)*
Martin Chamberlain
Henry Chitty
Ben Davis
James P. Dixon
William Engbretson
Elinor Greenberg
Archie Hargraves
  *(replaced 11/76 by Benjamin Alexander)*
Michiko Ishikawa
  *(replaced 11/76 by William Birenbaum)*
James Mullen
Jules Pagano
Carol Pollis
Milton Schwebel
Dorothy Williams
Robert Woodbury
Joseph Zepeda
  *(replaced 11/76 by Carole Esqueda)*

## MEMBERS OF THE BOARD OF TRUSTEES ——— 1977/1978

Trustees

Benjamin Alexander
William M. Birenbaum
Martin Chamberlain
King V. Cheek, *ex officio*
Jerry Cohen
Ben Davis
James P. Dixon, Chair, Board of Trustees
William Engbretson
Carlos Esqueda *(resigned May 1978)*
Elinor Greenberg
James Mullen *(resigned January 1978)*
Jules Pagano
Carol Pollis
Milton Schwebel
Dorothy Williams
Ronald Williams
Robert Woodbury

## MEMBERS OF THE BOARD OF TRUSTEES ——— 1978/1979

Trustees

Benjamin Alexander
Martin Chamberlain
William Engbretson
Leo Goodman-Malamuth
Edward Harris
Richard Hernandez
Robert Navarro
Samuel B. Ross
Kenneth W. Rothe, *ex officio*
Portia Holmes Shields
Pamela C. Spriggs
Karl Stauber
Ronald Williams
Ronald Woodbury

## MEMBERS OF THE BOARD OF TRUSTEES —— 1979/1980

| | |
|---|---|
| Trustees | Benjamin Alexander<br>Martin Chamberlain<br>William Engbretson<br>Leo Goodman-Malamuth<br>Edward Harris<br>Richard Hernandez<br>Robert Navarro<br>Samuel B. Ross<br>Kenneth W. Rothe, *ex officio*<br>Portia Holmes Shields<br>Pamela C. Spriggs<br>Karl Stauber<br>Ronald Williams<br>Robert Woodbury |

## MEMBERS OF THE BOARD OF TRUSTEES —— 1980/1981

| | |
|---|---|
| Trustees | Martin Chamberlain<br>Strachan Donnelley<br>Leo Goodman-Malamuth<br>Edward Harris<br>Richard Hernandez<br>George Korey<br>Samuel Ross<br>Kenneth W. Rothe, *ex officio*<br>Pamela C. Spriggs<br>Fay H. Williams<br>Ronald Williams<br>Robert Woodbury |

## MEMBERS OF THE BOARD OF TRUSTEES —— 1981/1982

Trustees
| John Blanton
John Brown
Martin Chamberlain *(resigned 1981)*
Strachan Donnelley
Edwina Gantz
Leo Goodman-Malamuth
Sidney Harman
Edward Harris
Richard Hernandez
George Korey
James Markley *(resigned 1982)*
Robert Oelman
Samuel Ross
Kenneth W. Rothe, *ex officio*
Frank Scott
Pamela Spriggs
Fay H. Williams
Ronald Williams
Robert Woodbury

## MEMBERS OF THE BOARD OF TRUSTEES —— 1982/1983

Trustees
| John Blanton
John Brown
Robert T. Conley, *ex officio*
Strachan Donnelley
Edwina Gantz
Leo Goodman-Malamuth
Sidney Harman
Edward Harris
George Korey
Robert Oelman
Samuel Ross
Frank Scott
Pamela Spriggs *(resigned 1983)*
Fay H. Williams
Ronald Williams
Robert Woodbury

## MEMBERS OF THE BOARD OF TRUSTEES —— 1983/1984

Trustees
| John Blanton
| John Brown
| Robert Conley, *ex officio*
| Strachan Donnelley
| Edwina Gantz
| Leo Goodman-Malamuth
| Sidney Harman
| Ed Harris
| George Korey
| Robert Oelman
| Samuel Ross
| Frank Scott
| Fay Williams
| Robert Woodbury
| Ronald Williams
| Robert Woodbury

## MEMBERS OF THE BOARD OF TRUSTEES —— 1984/1985

Trustees
| John Blanton
| John Brown
| Robert Brown
| Robert Conley, *ex officio*
| Strachan Donnelley
| Edwina Gantz
| Leo Goodman-Malamuth
| Sidney Harman
| Ed Harris
| George Korey
| George Kuser
| Diane Mosbacher
| Robert Oelman
| Samuel Ross
| Frank Scott
| Conrad Snowden
| Fay Williams
| Ronald Williams
| Robert Woodbury

## MEMBERS OF THE BOARD OF TRUSTEES —— 1985/1986

Trustees

John Blanton
John Brown
Robert Brown
Robert Conley, *ex officio*
Strachan Donnelley
Edwina Gantz
Leo Goodman-Malamuth
Sidney Harman
Ed Harris
George Korey
George Kuser
Diane Mosbacher
Robert Oelman
Samuel Ross
Frank Scott
Conrad Snowden
Fay Williams
Ronald Williams *(resigned 1985)*
Robert Woodbury

## MEMBERS OF THE BOARD OF TRUSTEES —— 1986/1987

Trustees

John Blanton
John Brown *(resigned 1986)*
Robert Brown
Robert Conley, *ex officio*
Strachan Donnelley
Edwina Gantz
Leo Goodman-Malamuth
Sidney Harman
Ed Harris
George Korey
George Kuser *(resigned 1986)*
Diane Mosbacher
Robert Oelman *(resigned 1986)*
Samuel Ross
Frank Scott *(resigned 1986)*
Conrad Snowden *(resigned 1986)*
Fay Williams
Robert Woodbury *(resigned 1986)*

## MEMBERS OF THE BOARD OF TRUSTEES —— 1987/1988

Trustees
: John Blanton
Robert Brown
Robert Conley, *ex officio*
Strachan Donnelley
Edwina Gantz
Alan Guskin
Leo Goodman-Malamuth
Sidney Harman
Ed Harris
George Korey
Diane Mosbacher
George Pruitt
Samuel Ross
Fay Williams

## MEMBERS OF THE BOARD OF TRUSTEES —— 1988/1989

Trustees
: John Blanton
Robert Brown
Robert Conley, *ex officio*
Strachan Donnelley
Edwina Gantz *(resigned 1988)*
Alan Guskin
Leo Goodman-Malamuth
Sidney Harman
Ed Harris
George Korey
Diane Mosbacher
Marysa Navarro
George Pruitt
Samuel Ross
Fay Williams

## MEMBERS OF THE BOARD OF TRUSTEES — 1989/1990

Trustees

John Blanton
Robert Brown
Robert Conley, *ex officio*
Strachan Donnelley
Alan Guskin
Leo Goodman-Malamuth
Sidney Harman
Ed Harris *(resigned 1989)*
Joanne Hayes
George Korey
Diane Mosbacher
Marysa Navarro
George Pruitt
Samuel Ross
Fay Williams

## MEMBERS OF THE BOARD OF TRUSTEES — 1990/1991

Trustees

John Blanton
Robert Brown
Robert Conley, *ex officio*
Strachan Donnelley
Alan Guskin
Leo Goodman-Malamuth
Sidney Harman
Joanne Hayes
George Korey
Diane Mosbacher
Marysa Navarro
George Pruitt
Samuel Ross *(resigned 1990)*
Fay Williams

## MEMBERS OF THE BOARD OF TRUSTEES —— 1991/1992

Trustees
| John Blanton
Robert Brown *(resigned 1991)*
Robert Conley, *ex officio*
Strachan Donnelley
Alan Guskin
Leo Goodman-Malamuth
Sidney Harman
Joanne Hayes
George Korey
Diane Mosbacher *(resigned 1991)*
Marysa Navarro
George Pruitt
Lincoln Ragsdale
Fay Williams

## MEMBERS OF THE BOARD OF TRUSTEES —— 1992/1993

Trustees
| John Blanton
Robert Conley, *ex officio*
Strachan Donnelley *(resigned 1992)*
Alan Guskin
Leo Goodman-Malamuth
Sidney Harman
Joanne Hayes
George Korey
Bruce McMahan
Marysa Navarro
George Pruitt
Lincoln Ragsdale
Fay Williams

## MEMBERS OF THE BOARD OF TRUSTEES —— 1993/1994

Trustees
: John Blanton
Robert Conley, *ex officio*
Alan Guskin
Leo Goodman-Malamuth
Sidney Harman
Joanne Hayes
George Korey
Bruce McMahan
Marysa Navarro
George Pruitt
Lincoln Ragsdale
Fay Williams

## MEMBERS OF THE BOARD OF TRUSTEES —— 1994/1995

Trustees
: John Blanton
Robert Conley, *ex officio*
Alan Guskin *(resigned 1994)*
Rad Ewing
Leo Goodman-Malamuth
Sidney Harman *(resigned 1994)*
Joanne Hayes
George Korey
Bruce McMahan
Marysa Navarro
George Pruitt
Lincoln Ragsdale
Fay Williams

## MEMBERS OF THE BOARD OF TRUSTEES —— 1995/1996

Trustees
: John Blanton
Robert Conley, *ex officio*
Rad Ewing
Leo Goodman-Malamuth
Joanne Hayes
George Korey
Bruce McMahan
Marysa Navarro
George Pruitt
Lincoln Ragsdale *(resigned 1995)*
Fay Williams

## MEMBERS OF THE BOARD OF TRUSTEES —— 1996/1997

| | |
|---|---|
| Trustees | John Blanton<br>Robert Conley, *ex officio*<br>Rad Ewing<br>Leo Goodman-Malamuth<br>Joanne Hayes<br>George Korey<br>Bruce McMahan<br>Marysa Navarro<br>George Pruitt<br>Fay Williams |

## MEMBERS OF THE BOARD OF TRUSTEES —— 1997/1998

| | |
|---|---|
| Trustees | John Blanton<br>Robert Conley, *ex officio*<br>Rad Ewing<br>Cheryl Foley<br>Leo Goodman-Malamuth<br>Joanne Hayes<br>George Korey<br>Bruce McMahan<br>Marysa Navarro<br>George Pruitt<br>Fay Williams |

## MEMBERS OF THE BOARD OF TRUSTEES —— 1998/1999

| | |
|---|---|
| Trustees | John Blanton<br>Robert Conley, *ex officio*<br>Rad Ewing<br>Cheryl Foley<br>Leo Goodman-Malamuth<br>Joanne Hayes<br>George Korey<br>Bruce McMahan<br>Marysa Navarro<br>George Pruitt<br>Fay Williams |

## MEMBERS OF THE BOARD OF TRUSTEES — 1999/2000

Trustees
| John Blanton *(resigned 1999)*
Merv Cadwallader, *ex officio*
Robert Conley, *ex officio*
Rad Ewing
Cheryl Foley
Leo Goodman-Malamuth
Joanne Hayes
George Korey
Bruce McMahan
Marysa Navarro
George Pruitt
Judith Sturnick, *ex officio*
Fay Williams

## MEMBERS OF THE BOARD OF TRUSTEES — 2000/2001

Trustees
| Clifford Bailey
Merv Cadwallader, *ex officio (resigned 2000)*
Rad Ewing
Cheryl Foley
Leo Goodman-Malamuth
Joanne Hayes
George Korey
Bruce McMahan
Marysa Navarro
Clarissa Pinkola-Estes
George Pruitt
Eugene Ruehlmann
Judith Sturnick, *ex officio*
Fay Williams *(resigned 2001)*

## Members of the Board of Trustees —— 2001/2002

Trustees

Clifford Bailey
Rad Ewing
Cheryl Foley
Leo Goodman-Malamuth
Joanne Hayes *(resigned 2001)*
George Korey
Bruce McMahan
Marysa Navarro
Clarissa Pinkola-Estes
George Pruitt
Eugene Ruehlmann
Judith Sturnick, *ex officio*

## Members of the Board of Trustees —— 2002/2003

Trustees

Richard Aft
Clifford Bailey
Rad Ewing
Cheryl Foley
Leo Goodman-Malamuth
George Korey
Bruce McMahan
Marysa Navarro
Clarissa Pinkola-Estes
George Pruitt
Eugene Ruehlmann
Judith Sturnick, *ex officio (resigned 2002)*
Roger Sublett, *ex officio*

## MEMBERS OF THE BOARD OF TRUSTEES —— 2003/2004

Trustees
: Richard Aft
Clifford Bailey
Rad Ewing
Cheryl Foley
Leo Goodman-Malamuth
George Korey
Lisa Lorimer
Bruce McMahan *(resigned 2003)*
Marysa Navarro
Clarissa Pinkola-Estes
George Pruitt
Eugene Ruehlmann
Barbara Scheuer
Roger Sublett, *ex officio*
Christine VanDuelmen

## MEMBERS OF THE BOARD OF TRUSTEES —— 2004/2005

Trustees
: Richard Aft
Clifford Bailey *(resigned 2004)*
Rad Ewing
Cheryl Foley
Leo Goodman-Malamuth
George Korey
Lisa Lorimer
Marysa Navarro *(resigned 2005)*
Clarissa Pinkola-Estes
George Pruitt
Eugene Ruehlmann
Barbara Scheuer *(resigned 2004)*
Roger Sublett, *ex officio*
Christine VanDuelmen
Gerald Von Deylen

## Members of the Board of Trustees —— 2005/2006

Trustees

Richard Aft
Martha Bidez
Rad Ewing
Cheryl Foley
Leo Goodman-Malamuth
George Korey
Lisa Lorimer
Clarissa Pinkola-Estes *(resigned 2006)*
George Pruitt
Eugene Ruehlmann *(resigned 2005)*
Roger Sublett, *ex officio*
Tab Turner *(resigned 2006)*
Christine VanDuelmen
Gerald Von Deylen
Virginia Wiltse

## Members of the Board of Trustees —— 2006/2007

Trustees

Richard Aft
Martha Bidez
Rad Ewing
Cheryl Foley
Thomas Gilman
Leo Goodman-Malamuth *(resigned 2007)*
Joel Kanter
Hanmin Liu
Lisa Lorimer
George Pruitt
Roger Sublett, *ex officio*
Christine VanDuelmen
Gerald Von Deylen *(resigned 2006)*
Virginia Wiltse

## MEMBERS OF THE BOARD OF TRUSTEES —— 2007/2008

| | |
|---|---|
| Trustees | Richard Aft<br>Martha Bidez<br>Rad Ewing<br>Cheryl Foley<br>Thomas Gilman<br>Michele Hunt<br>Joel Kanter<br>Hanmin Liu<br>Lisa Lorimer<br>George Pruitt<br>Larry Spears<br>Roger Sublett, *ex officio*<br>Christine VanDuelmen<br>Virginia Wiltse |

## MEMBERS OF THE BOARD OF TRUSTEES —— 2008/2009

| | |
|---|---|
| Trustees | Richard Aft<br>Martha Bidez<br>Rad Ewing *(resigned 2008)*<br>Cheryl Foley<br>Thomas Gilman<br>Michele Hunt<br>Joel Kanter<br>Hanmin Liu<br>Lisa Lorimer<br>George Pruitt<br>Blake Ratcliff<br>Larry Spears *(resigned 2008)*<br>Roger Sublett, *ex officio*<br>Maxine Thomas<br>Christine VanDuelmen<br>Virginia Wiltse |

## MEMBERS OF THE BOARD OF TRUSTEES ——— 2009/2010

Trustees

Richard Aft
Martha Bidez
Cheryl Foley
Thomas Gilman *(resigned 2010)*
Michele Hunt *(resigned 2010)*
Louis Jolivert
Joel Kanter
Hanmin Liu
Lisa Lorimer
Shekhar Mitra
George Pruitt
Matthew Quinn
Blake Ratcliff *(resigned 2010)*
Susan Robinson
Roger Sublett, *ex officio*
Maxine Thomas
Christine VanDuelmen
Virginia Wiltse

## MEMBERS OF THE BOARD OF TRUSTEES ——— 2010/2011

Trustees

Richard Aft
Martha Bidez
Don Feldmann
Cheryl Foley *(resigned 2011)*
Louis Jolivert *(resigned 2010)*
Joel Kanter
Hanmin Liu *(resigned 2010)*
Lisa Lorimer
Shekhar Mitra
Betty Overton-Adkins
George Pruitt *(resigned 2011)*
Matthew Quinn
Susan Robinson
Roger Sublett, *ex officio*
Maxine Thomas
Christine VanDuelmen
Virginia Wiltse

## MEMBERS OF THE BOARD OF TRUSTEES ——— 2011/2012

Trustees
| Richard Aft
Roger Allbee
Martha Bidez
Don Feldmann
Kay Goss
Gladys Hankins
Joel Kanter
Sandra Lobert
Lisa Lorimer *(resigned 2011)*
Shekhar Mitra
Betty Overton-Adkins
Susan Porter Robinson
Matthew Quinn *(resigned 2012)*
Roger Sublett, *ex officio*
Maxine Thomas *(resigned 2012)*
Christine VanDuelmen
Bruce Weinstein
Virginia Wiltse

## MEMBERS OF THE BOARD OF TRUSTEES ——— 2012/2013

Trustees
| Richard Aft
Roger Allbee
Martha Bidez *(resigned 2012)*
Don Feldmann
Kay Goss
Gladys Hankins
Joel Kanter *(resigned 2013)*
Sandra Lobert
Shekhar Mitra
Betty Overton-Adkins
Susan Porter Robinson *(resigned 2012)*
Katherine Prince
Roger Sublett, *ex officio*
Christine VanDuelmen
Bruce Weinstein
Virginia Wiltse

## MEMBERS OF THE BOARD OF TRUSTEES — 2013/2014

| | |
|---|---|
| Trustees | Richard Aft<br>Roger Allbee<br>Lee Binder<br>Juana Bordas<br>Don Feldmann<br>Kay Goss<br>Gladys Hankins<br>Sandra Lobert<br>Shekhar Mitra<br>Betty Overton-Adkins<br>Katherine Prince<br>Edgar Smith, Jr.<br>Roger Sublett, *ex officio*<br>Dennis Tartakow<br>Christine VanDuelmen<br>Bruce Weinstein *(resigned 2014)*<br>Virginia Wiltse |

## MEMBERS OF THE BOARD OF TRUSTEES — 2014/2015

| | |
|---|---|
| Trustees | Richard Aft<br>Roger Allbee<br>Lee Binder<br>Juana Bordas<br>Kim Byas<br>Don Feldmann<br>Kay Goss<br>Gladys Hankins<br>Sandra Lobert<br>Shekhar Mitra<br>Betty Overton-Adkins<br>Katherine Prince<br>Edgar Smith, Jr.<br>Roger Sublett, *ex officio*<br>Dennis Tartakow<br>Christine VanDuelmen<br>Virginia Wiltse *(resigned 2015)* |

# Bibliography

## *Articles and Books*

"About Vermont College." *The Network.* Summer 2001.

"The Accidental Scholar." *The Network.* Summer 1999.

"Among Colleges and Universities Professing to Teach Students How to Think." *Chicago Tribune,* July 25, 1965.

"The Anniversary Conference, Goddard College: Change and Challenge in Liberal Education." *Goddard Bulletin.* September 1963.

"Answering the Call: Cadwallader Moves from Professorship to Acting Presidency." *The Network,* Summer 1999.

Baskin, Samuel and E. F. Hallenbeck. "University Without Walls: Nontraditional Program of Undergraduate Learning." *Compact,* Oct. 1972.

Benson, Ann Giles and Frank Adams. *To Know for Real: Royce S. Pitkin and Goddard College.* Adamant, Vermont: Adamant Press, 1987.

"Best Colleges: All of the Rest." *U.S. News & World Report,* October 4, 1993.

"Board Approves Acquisition of Vermont College: Transition Planning Process Begins." *The Network,* Summer 2001.

Cappel, Constance, ed. *A Union of Voices: Accounts of the Union Institute & University.* XLibris: Graduate Alumnae/i Board of Union Institute & University, 2004.

Carlson, Scott. "Goddard College Takes a Highly Unconventional Path to Survival." *The Chronicle of Higher Education,* September 9, 2011.

"City Center for Experimental Education Studies." *Cincinnati Post,* August 24, 1977.

Collar, Kelly. "Getting to the Roots of Adult Education: A Conversation with Goddard's ADP Pioneer." *Clockworks.* Winter/Spring 2007.

"Deaths: Baskin, Dr. Samuel." *The New York Times*, May 23, 2002.

Dixon, Edla M., ed. *Antioch: The Dixon Era, 1959–1975. Perspectives of James P. Dixon.* Saco, Maine: Bastille Books, 1991.

Driehaus, Bob. "Fifty Years On, Union Institute & University Keeps Quietly Growing in Uptown." WCPO.Com, Accessed March 19, 2014.

Fairfield, Roy P. *Person-Centered Graduate Education.* Buffalo, NY: Prometheus Books, 1977.

Frothingham, Nat. "Vermont College and Union: One Plus One Equals Three." *Montpelier Bridge*, May 2001.

http://www.mtbytes.com/mpbridge/article.cfm?articleid=264.

Gay, Roger Crowell. *Nasson College (1912–1957): A Modern Parable of the Mustard Seed.* The Newcomen Address. Printed for the Newcomen Society .Princeton, NJ: Princeton University Press, 1958.

"Goddard at 25." *Newsweek,* April 8, 1963.

"Hartwick History." http://www.hartwick.edu/about-us/hartwick-history. Accessed February 13, 2014. Hendra, Rick and Ed Harris.

"Unpublished Results: The University Without Walls Experiment." Revised 2002. http://www-unix.oit.umass.edu/~hendra/Unpublished%20 Results.html. Accessed April 5, 2014.

Joy, Patrick. "Vermont College Alumni Group Makes Offer to Buy Campus." *The Rutland Herald*, November 1, 2006.
http://www.rutlandherald.com/apps/pbcs.dll/article?AID=/20061101/NEWS/61 1010392/1004/NEWS03.

Kirkhorn, Michael. "Union for Experimenting Colleges and Universities: Back from the Brink." *Change Magazine,* April 1979.

Kline, Reamer. *Education for the Common Good: A History of Bard College: The First 100 Years, 1860–1960.* Annandale-on-Hudson, New York: Bard College, 1982.

"Leo Goodman-Malamuth, Second GSU President, Dies at 88." Obituary. http://www.enewspf.com/latest-news/school-news/39801-leo-goodman-malamuth-second-gsu-president-dies-at-88.html

"Lighthouse Closes on Gruen Watch Co. Building." *Building Cincinnati*. January 22, 2009. http://www.building-cincinnati.com/2009/01/lighthouse-closes-on-gruen-watch-co.html.

*Measures of Enduring Excellence: Journeys Toward Greater Leadership & Service*. Scottsdale, AZ: New Education Press, 2010.

Milam, John H. *A History of Adult Education at Goddard College, 1938–1969*. M.A. Thesis, Goddard College, 1985.

"News from the Tower: Judith A. Sturnick named Fourth President of the Union Institute." *The Network*, Spring 2000.

"News from the Tower & Beyond: Board Approves Acquisition of Vermont College." *The Network*, Summer 2001.

Nichols, L. M., and Geoffrey T. Hellman. "The Talk of the Town: Singing Professor." *The New Yorker*, January 13, 1951.

"Open University is Born." *Science*, Vol. 171, No. 3974, March 15, 1971.

Ost, R. Thomas. "Robert T. Conley." *The Network*, Summer 1999.

"Our New Home: A Community Partnership." http://www.lys.org/documents/Summer09.pdf. Accessed August 20, 2014.

"Procter and Collier Company." http://www.cincinnativiews.net/suburban_buildings.htm. Accessed July 30, 2014.

"Procter and Collier Beau Brummell Building." http://www.examiner.com/article/procter-and-collier-beau-brummell-building. Accessed July 30, 2014.

"The Reamer Kline Years: An Appreciation." http://www.bard.edu/archives/voices/Kline-Education/Appreciation.pdf. Accessed February 12, 2014.

"Report of a Visit to the Union Institute, October 23–25, 1989." The Commission on Institutions of Higher Education of the North Central Association of Colleges and Schools, 1989.

"Report of a Visit to the University Without Walls." Commission on Institutions of Higher Education of the North Central Association of Colleges and Secondary Schools, May 1972.

"Rev. Dr. Reamer Kline Dies; Ex-President of Bard College." Obituary. *The New York Times*, March 10, 1983.

Rosenman, Mark. "Reasserting Charity's Value." *The Network*, Spring 1999.

"Jerome Sachs, 1914–2012." Obituary. *Chicago Tribune*, October 18, 2012.

"Seymour Smith." Obituary. *Toledo Blade,* September 6, 1995.

"Paul L. Ward, 94, Historian and College President, Dies." Obituary. *The New York Times,* November 18, 2005.

Sacks, Pamela H. "Montpelier Miracle: Novelist and Worcester native Thomas Greene Creates a New College." The *Worcester (*Mass.) *Telegram & Gazette*, July 15, 2008. http://www.telegram.com/article/20080715/NEWS/807150391/1102.

"Trustees Approve Budget, Tuition Hike, Nix Vt. College Purchase." Associated Press, May 21, 2006.

http://www.boston.com/news/education/higher/articles/2006/05/21/trustees_approve_budget_tuition_hike_nix_vt_college_purchase/.

"Union Institute & University Signs Letter of Intent to Sell Vermont College Campus to Vermont College of Fine Arts," February 26, 2007.

http://www.vermontbiz.com/news/february/union-institute-sell-vermont-college-campus.

"Universities: What Tearing Down the Walls Can Do." *The New York Times,* December 27, 1970.

"University Family Mourns President Robert T. Conley's Passing." *The Network*, Summer 1999.

Watkins, Steve. "The Sale-Leaseback: One Way to Unlock Equity." *Cincinnati Business Courier,* March 29, 2010.
http://www.bizjournals.com/cincinnati/stories/2010/03/29/story19.html.

## Author's Interviews

King V. Cheek. Interview (telephone) by Benjamin Justesen. April 3, 2014.

Doris Conley. Interview by Benjamin Justesen, Cincinnati, OH. April 10, 2014.

Cheryl Foley. Interview (telephone) by Benjamin Justesen. April 10, 2014.

Lisa Lorimer. Interview (telephone) by Benjamin Justesen. April 8, 2014.

Betty Overton-Adkins. Interview (telephone) by Benjamin Justesen. April 10, 2014.

George A. Pruitt. Interview (telephone) by Benjamin Justesen. May 7, 2014.

Kenneth W. Rothe. Interview by Benjamin Justesen, Cincinnati, OH. April 9, 2014.

Helena Judith Sturnick. Interview (telephone) by Benjamin Justesen. April 15, 2014.

Roger H. Sublett. Interview (telephone) by Benjamin Justesen. October 3, 2014.

Roger H. Sublett. Interview (telephone) by Benjamin Justesen. February 12, 2015.

## Press Releases

"Baskin to Leave Union Presidency to Head New UECU Institute for Research and Program Development. King Cheek Chosen as Successor." Union for Experimenting Colleges and Universities, Yellow Springs, OH. April 28, 1976.

Goddard College News. Plainfield, VT. February 27, 1965.

"King Cheek New UECU Vice President." Union for Experimenting Colleges and Universities, Yellow Springs, OH. July 11, 1974.

The Ford Foundation. February 16, 1971.

Union for Research and Experimentation in Higher Education, Yellow Springs, OH. October 31, 1967.

Union for Experimenting Colleges and Universities, Yellow Springs, OH. February 6, 1970.

UREHE. Yellow Springs, OH. October 31, 1967.

"University Without Walls Program Receives Pre-Accreditation." Union for Experimenting Colleges and Universities. September 5, 1972.

## *Institutional Publications*

"A Brief History of the Union Institute." The Union Institute, Cincinnati, OH. Draft, February 1998.

"A Special Report from the President". The Union for Experimenting Colleges and Universities, Cincinnati, OH. March 15, 1989.

"About Goddard," www.goddard.edu. Accessed January 30, 2014.

"About NCF: A College Ahead of its Time." http://www.ncf.edu/history. Accessed April 5, 2014.

"Announcement: Union Graduate School." Union for Experimenting Colleges and Universities, Yellow Springs, OH. January 1970.

"Charge to the Union Graduate School Reorganization Committee." Memorandum from King V. Cheek, President, to UGS Reorganization Committee. Union for Experimenting Colleges and Universities, Cincinnati, OH. March 8, 1978.

"CHU Campus and History." http://www.chu.edu/index.php/whychu/chu-campus.html. Accessed April 5, 2014.

"Engage, Enlighten, Empower: A Report from President Roger H. Sublett and the Board of Trustees, July 2007–June 2009."Union Institute & University, Cincinnati, OH, 2009.

*50th Anniversary, Union Institute & University, 1964–2014*. Union Institute & University, Cincinnati, OH, 2014.

"History: Overview." Ford Foundation. http://www.fordfoundation.org/about-us/history. Accessed April 4, 2014.

"History of Nasson College." http://www.nasson.org/HISTORY.html. Accessed March 30, 2014.

*Institutional Self Study, Vol. 1*. The Union for Experimenting Colleges and Universities Cincinnati, OH, 1984.

"Journeying: A Brief History of the Union Institute." Draft. Union Institute & University Archives, Cincinnati, OH. October 14, 1996.

The Kettering Foundation. "Our History." http://kettering.org/who-we-are/history/. Accessed April 4, 2014.

Lord, Gary Thomas. "Norwich University." 1995. http://www.norwich.edu/about/history.html.

Memorandum to the UECU Community from King V. Cheek, President. Cincinnati, OH. January 20, 1978.

"Notable Alumni." Union Institute & University. http://www.myunion.edu/FiftyYears/Notables.aspx. Accessed April 10, 2014.

"President's Report: 1998—first draft, March 1998." Transcription of an oral interview by Anu Mitra with Bob Conley, in the Union Institute & University Archives, Cincinnati, OH.

"Reorganization Plan, Approved January 1979." Cincinnati, OH: The Union for Experimenting Colleges and Universities, 1979.

"Report of the President of UECU, King V. Cheek." Cincinnati, OH. January 1978. "A Self Study of the Union for Experimenting Colleges and Universities." Union for Experimenting Colleges and Universities, Cincinnati, OH. September 1980.

"Seton Hall University: A Brief History." http://www.shu.edu/academics/libraries/archives/shu-history.cfm.

"Union Graduate School: Current Developments." Memorandum from Roy Fairfield and Goodwin Watson, February 16, 1970.

"Union Institute Ranked Among the Best in *U.S. News & World Report* Survey." Union Institute flyer, printed in October 1993. The Union Institute, Cincinnati, OH, 1993.

"Who Was Ronald Williams?" http://library.neiu.edu/aboutthelibrary/ronaldwilliams.html. Accessed August 30, 2014.

## *Private Papers*

Conley, Robyn. Remarks at ceremony naming the Union Institute Academic Building for Robert T. Conley, 2001. Private copy of tribute provided by Doris Conley.

# Endnotes

[1] Forest K. Davis, *Things Were Different in Royce's Day: Royce S. Pitkin as Progressive Educator: A Perspective from Goddard College, 1950–1967* (Adamant Press, 1996), 110–122.

[2] Scott Carlson, "Goddard College Takes a Highly Unconventional Path to Survival," *The Chronicle of Higher Education* (September 9, 2011).

[3] Davis, *Things were Different in Royce's Day*, 110.

[4] "About Goddard," www.goddard.edu. Accessed January 30, 2014.

[5] Kelly Collar, "Getting to the Roots of Adult Education: A Conversation with Goddard's ADP Pioneer," *Clockworks* (Winter/Spring 2007), 7-8. Bates, semi-retired at age 90, had outlived Pitkin by more than 20 years, but was still energetically pushing their educational agenda in this interview.

[6] Collar, "Getting to the Roots," 7.

[7] Carlson, "Goddard College."

[8] *Goddard College News,* February 27, 1965 [Press release].

[9] Ann Giles Benson and Frank Adams, *To Know for Real: Royce S. Pitkin and Goddard College* (Adamant Press, 1987), 207.

[10] Kelly Collar, "Getting to the Roots of Adult Education: A Conversation with Goddard's ADP Pioneer," *Clockworks* (Winter/Spring 2007), 7.

[11] John H. Milam, "A History of Adult Education at Goddard College, 1938-1969," M.A. thesis, Goddard College, 1985), 23. The New Jersey group included the state's colleges at Glassboro, Jersey City, Montclair, Newark, Trenton, and Wayne, all since renamed.

[12] Ibid.

[13] "Goddard at 25," *Newsweek,* April 8, 1963, 26. According to Benson and Adams (*To Know for Real*, 190), Pitkin recalled inviting representatives of just eight schools—Antioch, Bard, Bennington, Monteith, New College, Reed, Sarah Lawrence, and Stephens—all of which reported on experimentation at their campuses. This same list appeared in the bulletin for "The Anniversary Conference, Goddard College: Change and Challenge in Liberal Education" (*Goddard Bulletin*, September 1963). Other schools represented at the conference did not make formal presentations; their names were listed in a 1985 master's thesis by John Milam ("A History of Adult Education at Goddard College, 1938-1969," 23).

[14] "Goddard at 25."

[15] Benson and Adams, *To Know for Real*, 190.

[16] Ibid.

[17] Benson and Adams, *To Know for Real*, 208

[18] Ibid.

[19] Ibid.

[20] Ibid, 190, 208.

[21] *Goddard College News*, February 27, 1965, [Press release].

[22] Benson and Adams, *To Know for Real*, 209.

[23] Ibid.

[24] Milam, "A History of Adult Education at Goddard," 24. The "Organizing Conference of the Union for Research and Experimentation in Higher Education" took place in Plainfield on February 26-28, 1965, and was chaired by Harry ("Mike") Giles of NYU.

[25] The Chicago school would soon change its name. In 1965, the state of Illinois renamed it Illinois Teachers College: Chicago North; and in 1967, its name was changed to Northeastern Illinois State College. Since 1971, it has been known as Northeastern Illinois University.

[26] *Goddard College News,* February 27, 1965 [Press release].

[27] Ibid.

[28] Benson and Adams, *To Know for Real*, 209.

[29] "History," http://www.nasson.org/HISTORY.html. The reinvented Nasson College initially prospered, enrolling about 900 students by 1968, but then lost momentum. It shut down in 1983. The spirit of Nasson was kept alive through several reincarnations, including the distance-learning Sanford Center of the University of Maine, which closed in 2008.

30 Milam, "A History of Adult Education at Goddard,"24.

31 "Among colleges and universities professing to teach students how to think, little Shimer, 128 miles north-west of Chicago, succeeds like almost no place else," *Chicago Tribune*, July 25, 1965; "F. Joseph Mullin," *Chicago Tribune*, February 18, 1997.

32 "The Reamer Kline Years: An Appreciation," at http://www.bard.edu/archives/voices/Kline-Education/Appreciation.pdf, accessed February 12, 2014; "Rev. Dr. Reamer Kline Dies; Ex-President of Bard College," *New York Times*, March 10, 1983.

33 "Seymour Smith," *Toledo Blade*, September 6, 1995..

34 "Jerome Sachs, 1914-2012," *Chicago Tribune*, October 18, 2012.

35 L. M. Nichols and Geoffrey T. Hellman, "The Talk of the Town: Singing Professor." *The New Yorker*, January 13, 1951, 18.

36 "Paul L. Ward, 94, Historian and College President, Dies," *New York Times*, November 18, 2005.

37 *Goddard College News,* February 27, 1965 [Press release].

38 Ibid.

39 "Sam Baskin – Founder and First President of Union Institute & University," *Inside Union,* October 1, 2009. http://magazine.myunion.edu/?p=1958, accessed March 30, 2014.

40 Benson and Adams, *To Know for Real*, 267.

41 Ibid, 210.

42 Ibid.

43 King V. Cheek, Interview with Benjamin R. Justesen, April 3, 2014.

44 The most complete history of the school is Reamer Kline's *Education for the Common Good: A History of Bard College: The First 100 Years, 1860-1960* (Annandale-On-Hudson, NY: Bard College, 1982).

45 Benson and Adams, *To Know for Real*, 210.

46 Ibid., 267.

47 The Union for Experimenting Colleges and Universities. *Institutional Self Study, Vol. 1.* Cincinnati, Ohio, 1984, 27.

[48] "Background and need: Project Changeover," in an undated (1970?) UREHE report titled "Nurturing Innovation: A proposal to develop a nationwide network of Centers and Workshops for constructive innovation in higher education."

[49] News release, New College, Sarasota, Florida, November 2, 1967. http://ncf.sobek.ufl.edu/NCF0000668/00001., accessed April 15, 2015.

[50] The Kettering Foundation. "Our history," http://kettering.org/who-we-are/history/ >, accessed April 4, 2014.

[51] "History: Overview." The Ford Foundation web site. In a 1950 report to the public, the foundation listed five major goals of its philanthropy, including "Strengthen, expand and improve educational facilities and methods to enable individuals to realize more fully their intellectual, civic and spiritual potential; to promote greater equality of educational opportunity; and to conserve and increase knowledge and enrich our culture." http://www.fordfoundation.org/about-us/history, accessed April 4, 2014.

[52] King V. Cheek, Interview with Benjamin R. Justesen, April 3, 2014.

[53] Rick Hendra and Ed Harris, "Unpublished Results: The University Without Walls Experiment," for the University of Massachusetts, revised 2002. http://www-unix.oit.umass.edu/~hendra/Unpublished%20 Results.html, accessed April 5, 2014.

[54] Hendra and Harris, "Unpublished Results: University Without Walls Experiment."

[55] Samuel Baskin and E. F. Hallenbeck, "University Without Walls: Nontraditional Program of Undergraduate Learning," *Compact* (Oct. 1972): 21–25.

[56] Hendra and Harris, "Unpublished Results: University Without Walls Experiment," The list shown here includes text from a similar but extended list published in *UWW: A First Year Report,* The Union for Experimenting Colleges and Universities, Yellow Springs, OH, 1972.

[57] Ford Foundation, News release, February 16, 1971.

[58] Fred Hechinger, "Universities: What Tearing Down the 'Walls' Can Do," *The New York Times,* December 27, 1970.

[59] "Report of a Visit to the University Without Walls," Commission on Institutions of Higher Education of the North Central Association of Colleges and Secondary Schools, May 1972, 2.

[60] "Open University is Born," *Science*, Vol. 171, No. 3974, (March 5, 1971): 881.

[61] Ibid.

[62] Hendra and Harris, "Unpublished Results: University Without Walls Experiment."

[63] The larger figure is from "Unpublished Results," by Hendra and Harris: "By 1976 … [T]he fifty UWW programs were all underway in varying degrees of affiliation with the UECU."

[64] Michael Kirkhorn, "Union for Experimenting Colleges and Universities: Back from the Brink," *Change Magazine*, April 1979: 18–21.

[65] "University Without Walls Program Receives Pre-Accreditation," Union for Experimenting Colleges and Universities, News release, September 5, 1972.

[66] Ibid.

[67] "Report of a Visit to the University Without Walls," 9.

[68] Ibid., 9.

[69] Ibid., 10.

[70] Ibid., 11.

[71] "Union Graduate School: Current Developments," Memorandum, Yellow Springs, OH, from Roy Fairfield and Goodwin Watson, February 16, 1970.

[72] "The Union and Its Mission," Chapter 3, in *A Self Study of the Union for Experimenting Colleges and Universities*, (September 1980): 7.

[73] "Announcement: Union Graduate School," January 1970. The mimeographed memorandum, unsigned but later attributed to Sam Baskin, describes the characteristics of the final PhD program. It is the earliest written description of the UGS program that could be found in Union Institute files.

[74] "Union Graduate School: Current Developments," Ibid.

[75] "Notable Alumni," from Union Institute & University web site, http://www.myunion.edu/FiftyYears/Notables.aspx, accessed April 10, 2014.

[76] "A College Ahead of Its Time," Union for Research and Experimentation in Higher Education, October 31, 1967; http://www.ncf.edu/history, accessed April 5, 2014; "CHU Campus and History, http://www.chu.edu/index.php/whychu/chu-campus.html, accessed April 5, 2014. New College later became a part of the Florida public system of higher education. Loretto Heights, purchased in 1990 by a Japanese university group, is now known as Colorado Heights University.

[77] Union for Experimenting Colleges and Universities, Yellow Springs, Ohio, News release, February 6, 1970.

[78] "Report of a Visit to the University Without Walls." The report listed five (unnamed) members as joining in late 1971, bringing the total UECU membership to 22; the UECU news release in September 1972 listed 25 members, indicating that three more schools had joined since that visit.

79 No separate news releases announcing dates of memberships for these members were found in Union files.

80 "Union Adds Six," Union for Experimenting Colleges and Universities, News release, June 10, 1974.

81 "UECU Update," Union for Experimenting Colleges and Universities, Yellow Springs, Ohio, April 1975.

82 "Baskin to leave Union Presidency to Head New UECU Institute for Research and Program Development. King Cheek Chosen as Successor," Union for Experimenting Colleges and Universities, news release, April 28, 1976.

83 Ibid.

84 Ibid.

85 Ibid.

86 Ibid. Watson died in 1976, shortly after Baskin's announcement.

87 Ibid.

88 "King Cheek new UECU Vice President," Union for Experimenting Colleges and Universities, Yellow Springs, Ohio, Press release, July 11, 1974.

89 King Cheek, Interview with Benjamin R. Justesen, April 3, 2014.

90 King Cheek interview, ibid.

91 "City Center for Experimental Education Studies," *Cincinnati Post,* August 24, 1977.

92 Ibid.

93 Report of the President of UECU, King V. Cheek, Cincinnati, Ohio, January 1978.

94 Ibid.

95 Ibid.

96 The UECU files contain a sample of sharply worded letters from students, many written on the memorandum itself announcing the tuition hike.

97 "Charge to the Union Graduate School Reorganization Committee," Union for Experimenting Colleges and Universities, Cincinnati, Ohio. Memorandum from King V. Cheek, President, to UGS Reorganization Committee, March 8, 1978. Members of the committee included Jean Thomas Griffin, Rita Arditti, Chuck Sells, Warren Buford, Linn Jones, Ron Arroyo, Bob Atkins, C. T. Vivian, Jerry Mandina, and Joe Henriquez.

[98] Ben Davis, Interview by Ken Byers, May 1999, in *A Union of Voices: Accounts of the Union Institute & University,* Constance Cappel, editor (XLibris, 2004), 284–285.

[99] King Cheek, interview, April 3, 2014.

[100] Ben Davis, Interview by Ken Byers, May 1999, in *A Union of Voices*, 285.

[101] King Cheek interview, ibid.

[102] Ibid.

[103] "The Union for Research and Experimentation in Higher Education," in *Antioch: The Dixon Era, 1959–1975. Perspectives of James P. Dixon,* compiled and edited by Edla M. Dixon (Saco, Maine: Bastille Books, 1991), 175–185.

[104] Ibid, 186.

[105] Ben Davis, Interview by Ken Byers, May 1999.

[106] Michael Kirkhorn, "Back from the Brink," *Change*, 18.

[107] Kenneth W. Rothe, Interview with Benjamin R. Justesen, April 9, 2014.

[108] Ibid.

[109] Spiegel was a partner in the prominent Cincinnati law firm of Cohen, Todd, Kite & Spiegel.

[110] Kenneth W. Rothe, Interview with Benjamin R. Justesen, April 9, 2014.

[111] Michael Kirkhorn, "Back from the Brink," *Change*, 18.

[112] Ibid.

[113] Ibid., 19.

[114] Ibid.

[115] Ibid.

[116] Kenneth W. Rothe, Interview with Benjamin R. Justesen, April 9, 2014.

[117] Reorganization Plan, The Union for Experimenting Colleges and Universities, Cincinnati, OH; Approved: January 1979, iii.

[118] Ibid., iv.

[119] Ibid., vii, 2–7.

[120] "Seton Hall University: A Brief History," http://www.shu.edu/academics/libraries/archives/shu-history.cfm .

[121] Doris Conley, Interview with Benjamin R. Justesen, April 10, 2014.

[122] Robyn Conley's remarks, at ceremony naming the Union Institute Academic Building for Robert T. Conley, 2001.

[123] Doris Conley, Interview with Benjamin R. Justesen, April 10, 2014.

[124] "The Accidental Scholar," *The Network,* Summer 1999.

[125] Doris Conley, interview, ibid.

[126] Ibid.

[127] "Report of a Visit to the Union Institute, October 23–25, 1989," The Commission on Institutions of Higher Education of the North Central Association of Colleges and Schools, 1989, 12.

[128] "A Brief History of the Union Institute," Union Institute, Cincinnati, Ohio, drafted in February 1998.

[129] "Enrollments and Growth," in *A Special Report from the President,* The Union for Experimenting Colleges and Universities, Cincinnati, Ohio, March 15, 1989, 4.

[130] "Report of a Visit to the Union Institute, October 23–25, 1989," 16–17.

[131] "Procter and Collier Company," at http://www.cincinnativiews.net/suburban_buildings.htm. Accessed July 30, 2014.

[132] "Report of a Visit to the Union Institute, October 23-25, 1989," 17.

[133] "Procter and Collier Beau Brummell Building," at http://www.examiner.com/article/procter-and-collier-beau-brummell-building. Accessed July 30, 2014.

[134] Robyn Conley's remarks, ceremony naming the Academic Building for Robert T. Conley, 2001.

[135] "President's Report: 1998—first draft, March 1998," oral interview of Bob Conley by Anu Mitra, audiotape transcription in the Union Institute & University archives, Cincinnati, OH.

[136] Mark Rosenman, "Reasserting Charity's Value," in *The Network*, Spring 1999, 39; Dr. Ed Wingard interview by Gary Buehler in *A Union of Voices*, 149–150.

[137] "Journeying: A Brief History of the Union Institute," draft dated October 14, 1996, in the Union Institute & University archives; "Key Dates: The Union Institute," in the Union Institute & University archives, Cincinnati, OH.

[138] "Best Colleges: All of the Rest," *U.S. News & World Report*, October 4, 1993: 116–118.

[139] "Union Institute Ranked Among the Best in *U.S. News & World Report* Survey," Union Institute flyer, printed in October 1993.

[140] "Our New Home: A Community Partnership," at http://www.lys.org/documents/Summer09.pdf.

[141] "A Brief History of the Union Institute," February 1988.

[142] Doris Conley, interview, ibid.

[143] "University Family Mourns President Robert T. Conley's Passing," in *The Network*, Summer 1999: 4.

[144] Thomas R. Ost, ."Robert T. Conley," in *The Network*, Summer 1999.

[145] "President's Report: 1998—first draft, March 1998," oral interview of Bob Conley by Anu Mitra, audiotape transcription.

[146] "University Family Mourns President Robert T. Conley's Passing," *The Network*,2.

[147] "Answering the Call: Cadwallader Moves from Professorship to Acting Presidency," *The Network*, Summer 1999: 2-5.

[148] Ibid.

[149] Ibid.

[150] "News from the Tower: Judith A. Sturnick named Fourth President of the Union Institute," *The Network*, Spring 2000: 2.

[151] Ibid.

[152] "News from the Tower & Beyond: Board Approves Acquisition of Vermont College," *The Network*, Summer 2001: 4.

[153] Helena Judith Sturnick, Interview with Benjamin R. Justesen, April 15, 2014.

[154] Nat Frothingham, "Vermont College and Union: One Plus One Equals Three," *Montpelier Bridge,* May 2001. http://www.mtbytes.com/mpbridge/article.cfm?articleid=264.

[155] Gary Thomas Lord, "Norwich University," 1995, extract from http://www.norwich.edu/about/history.html.

[156] "About Vermont College," *Network*, Summer 2001: 3.

[157] Ibid.

[158] Nat Frothingham, "Vermont College and Union."

[159] "Board Approves Acquisition of Vermont College: Transition Planning Process Begins." *The Network*, Summer 2001: 4.

[160] Nat Frothingham, "Vermont College and Union." This extract comes from the text of the letter as reprinted here.

[161] Helena Judith Sturnick, Interview, ibid.

[162] Ibid.

[163] George Pruitt, Interview with Benjamin R. Justesen, May 7, 2014.

[164] Helena Judith Sturnick, Interview, ibid.

[165] George Pruitt, Interview with Benjamin R. Justesen, ibid.

[166] Ibid.

[167] Ibid.

[168] Ibid.

[169] Cheryl Foley, Interview with Benjamin R. Justesen, April 9, 2014.

[170] Ibid.

[171] Roger Sublett, Interview with Benjamin R. Justesen, February 12, 2015.

[172] Roger Sublett, Interview with Benjamin R. Justesen, October 3, 2014.

[173] Roger Sublett, Interview with Benjamin R Justesen, February 12, 2015.

[174] "What we do," Kellogg Foundation website, http://www.wkkf.org/what-we-do/overview. According to the Kellogg website: "We believe that one measure of a society is the importance it places on the optimal development of all of its children. We envision a future and a society where every child thrives, and we invest in areas to advance that vision."

[175] Roger Sublett, Interview, October 3, 2014.

[176] Ibid.

[177] Ibid.

[178] Lisa Lorimer, Interview with Benjamin R. Justesen, April 8, 2014.

[179] Ibid.

[180] Betty Overton-Adkins, interview with Benjamin Justesen, April 8, 2014.

[181] Roger Sublett, interview, October 3, 2014.

[182] Roger Sublett, interview, February 12, 2015.

[183] Ibid.

[184] Ibid.

[185] Ibid.

[186] Ibid. Turner's 1893 paper, "The Significance of the Frontier in American History," was delivered at a meeting of historians in Chicago and remains among the most famous academic works of the nineteenth century.

[187] "A Report from the President, Roger H. Sublett, PhD," in *Engage, Enlighten, Empower: A Report from President Roger H. Sublett and the Board of Trustees, July 2007–June 2009*. Union Institute & University, Cincinnati, Ohio, 2009: 9.

[188] "Trustees Approve Budget, Tuition Hike, Nix Vt. College Purchase," Associated Press, May 21, 2006. http://www.boston.com/news/education/higher/articles/2006/05/21/trustees_approve_budget_tuition_hike_nix_vt_college_purchase/.

[189] Ibid.

[190] Patrick Joy, "Vermont College Alumni Group Makes Offer to Buy Campus," *The Rutland Herald*, November 1, 2006. http://www.rutlandherald.com/apps/pbcs.dll/article?AID=/20061101/NEWS/611010392/1004/NEWS03.

[191] "Union Institute & University Signs Letter of Intent to Sell Vermont College Campus to Vermont College of Fine Arts," *Vermont Business Magazine*, February 26, 2007. http://www.vermontbiz.com/news/february/union-institute-sell-vermont-college-campus.

[192] Ibid.

[193] Pamela H. Sacks, "Montpelier Miracle: Novelist and Worcester Native Thomas Greene Creates a New College," *The Worcester (*Mass.) *Telegram & Gazette*, July 15, 2008. http://www.telegram.com/article/20080715/NEWS/807150391/1102.

[194] Kevin LeMaster, "Lighthouse Closes on Gruen Watch Co. Building," *Building Cincinnati,* January 22, 2009. http://www.building-cincinnati.com/2009/01/lighthouse-closes-on-gruen-watch-co.html.

[195] Steve Watkins, "The Sale-Leaseback: One Way to Unlock Equity," *Cincinnati Business Courier,* March 29, 2010. http://www.bizjournals.com/cincinnati/stories/2010/03/29/story19.html.

[196] Bob Driehaus, "Fifty Years On, Union Institute & University Keeps Quietly Growing in Uptown,"WCPO.com, March 19, 2014. http://www.wcpo.com/news/education/fifty-years-on-union-institute-university-keeps-quietly-growing-in-uptown.

[197] Roger Sublett, interview, February 12, 2015.

[198] Figures and program descriptions, as listed in *50<sup>th</sup> Anniversary, Union Institute & University, 1964–2014*, Union Institute & University, Cincinnati, Ohio, 2014, and "Winter Semester 2014–2015 Full-Time Equivalency as of January 29, 2015," a memorandum provided by Union Institute & University.

[199] Roger Sublett, interview, October 3, 2014.

[200] Ibid.

[201] Roger Sublett, interview, February 12, 2015.

[202] Ibid.

[203] Ibid.

[204] Ibid.

[205] Summary of excerpts from keynote address by President Roger Sublett, October 17, 2009, in *Measures of Enduring Excellence: Journeys Toward Greater Leadership & Service,* New Education Press: Scottsdale, AZ, 2010: i-xi.

[206] "A Report from the President, Roger H. Sublett, PhD"

[207] Roger Sublett, interview, February 12, 2015.

*About the Author*

**BENJAMIN R. JUSTESEN**

Union Institute & University alumnus Benjamin Justesen (PhD, 2009) works as an editor in Alexandria, Virginia. A former journalist and teacher, he is also a graduate of the University of North Carolina at Chapel Hill. His published books include *George Henry White: An Even Chance in the Race of Life* (2001).

www.ingramcontent.com/pod-product-compliance
Lightning Source LLC
LaVergne TN
LVHW020927090426
835512LV00020B/3251